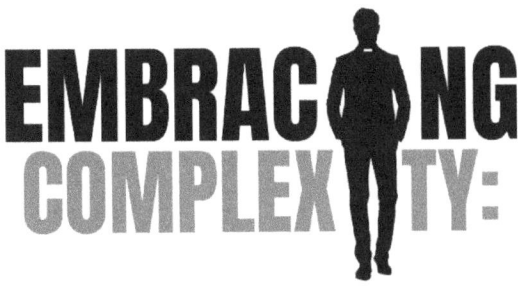

EMBRACING COMPLEXITY:

A BISHOP'S JOURNEY THROUGH LIFE,
FAITH, AND RESILIENCE

DR. DAVID E. TOMPKINS, SR.

ISBN: 979-8-9884486-7-9

Publishing By: DemiCo National, LLC

www.DemiCoNational.com

Table of Contents

Dedication Page

I wholeheartedly dedicate this book to the Living Word of Deliverance Temple Worship Center, a congregation that has been my source of inspiration and strength throughout my journey as a leader. To every member who has served under my guidance, your dedication and commitment have shaped my ministry and my life. It is my fervent hope that the words within these pages touch your hearts and inspire each of you to continue growing as individuals and believers.

To my beloved son, David Edward Tompkins, Jr., this book carries with it the essence of my aspirations for your future. May it serve as a testament to the values and principles that guide us, and may it inspire you to live a life of purpose, kindness, and loved, and my wife Slyvia Williams Tompkins, for being a lifetime supporter of my ministry.

Throughout the process of writing this book, I've held close to the mantra, 'just let it play out.' My dear congregants will recognize the significance of these words, knowing that life's complexities often unfold in unexpected ways, revealing profound lessons.

I extend my deepest gratitude to Mr. Johnny Brow, who directed me when I was just an eleven-year-old boy. Though he has since passed away, his guidance continues to influence my journey. I'd also like to express my appreciation to Dr. Anthony Dayse, whose unwavering support and inspiration have been instrumental in bringing this book to life.

This book is also a tribute to my beloved parents, Mozell Cartledge Tompkins and Marion Tompkins, whose love and guidance have been my foundation. I carry your legacy with pride and gratitude.

To my brothers, Larry Brown Tompkins, Curtis Lee Tompkins, and the late Dr. Charles Micheal Tompkins, and Willie Arthur Tompkins, Sr , I dedicate this work as a testament to the bonds that tie us together, transcending time and distance.

And lastly, I offer a heartfelt tribute to one of our most revered matriarchs, Mother Margie Helen Hooper, who now rests in Heaven. Her legacy of faith, love, and grace will forever be cherished within the walls of our church.

May this book serve as a beacon of hope, wisdom, and inspiration to all who read it, just as you have all been a source of strength and light in my life.

-Dr. David E. Tompkins, Sr.

.

Introduction

From a small town in McCormick, South Carolina to the sacred halls of faith, is where there is divine, and the human converge. Bishop Dr. David E. Tompkins found a profound perspective on life's intricate tapestry. Through the lens of his unwavering devotion to God, he has traversed the turbulent terrains of business, religion, relationships, friendships, the ministry, and the unfathomable depths of brokenness and resilience as he shares his experiences as a pastor of a non-denominational church and entrepreneur.

Dr. Tompkins' life exemplifies how the Complexity Form of Life weaves through the very fabric of existence, connecting the threads of business, religion, relationships, friendships, ministry, and the unyielding spirit in brokenness. As we embark on this spiritual voyage, may his experiences and reflections serve as guiding lights, illuminating our own paths as we seek purpose, understanding, and solace in a world that often defies our comprehension.

In the pages that follow, we shall witness life's grand tapestry unfolding, and in doing so, embrace the enigmatic beauty of the Complexity Form that shapes us all. Let us walk this journey together, as seekers of truth, stewards of love, and believers in the resiliency of the human spirit.

This book is an invitation to join him on a transformative odyssey, as we explore the Complexity Form of Life from the distant past to the enigmatic present with real situations, stories, and encouragement to continue the cause. Here's a summary of what lies ahead:

Overview of Sections

Section I: Complexity in Business –
Navigating the Corporate Crossroads

From the humble beginnings of a small town in McCormick, South Carolina, Bishop Dr. David E. Tompkins embarked on a remarkable journey that led him to the dynamic world of entrepreneurship. As we delve into the complexities of business, we uncover how his unwavering faith became the guiding force in navigating the corporate crossroads. Through the highs and lows of his entrepreneurial ventures, we will witness the delicate balance he sought between worldly pursuits and spiritual convictions.

His experiences will shed light on the ethical dilemmas, triumphs, and sacrifices that come with intertwining business acumen with a steadfast commitment to serving God and humanity.

Section II: Complexity in Religion –
Faith Woven in Time

The sacred halls of faith beckoned Bishop Tompkins, embracing him with timeless wisdom and divine revelations. In this segment, we shall embark on a journey through the annals of religious history, witnessing how his profound faith shaped his perspectives on morality, justice, and compassion. As we explore the intricacies of religious traditions, sacred scriptures, and the evolution of faith, we will come to understand how Bishop Tompkins' unwavering devotion provided solace and inspiration throughout his life, becoming the bedrock of his ministry.

Section III: Complexity in Relationships and
Friendships - Threads of Love and Trust

Central to Bishop Tompkins' ministry was a profound appreciation for the intricate threads of love and trust that bind humanity together. In this section, we will delve into the depths of relationships and friendships, uncovering the transformative power of empathy, forgiveness, and unconditional love. Through personal anecdotes and pastoral experiences, we will discover how he nurtured profound connections and how he helped others mend the broken pieces of their relationships.

Section IV: Complexity in the Ministry –
Nurturing Souls, Embracing Humanity

As a pastor of a non-denominational church, Bishop Tompkins bore the sacred responsibility of guiding souls and embracing the diverse tapestry of humanity. This segment will illuminate the challenges and joys of the ministry, exploring how his devotion to God translated into dedicated service to his congregation. From officiating sacred ceremonies to providing spiritual support during times of crisis, his experiences will reveal the profound impact of faith and compassion on the lives of those he touched.

Section V: Complexity in Brokenness and Resilience -
The Unyielding Spirit

Life's journey seldom unfolds without moments of profound brokenness. In this closing section, we will bear witness to Bishop Tompkins' own trials and tribulations, and how he navigated the darkest corners of despair. Through his indomitable spirit and unwavering faith, he emerged as a beacon of hope and resilience, inspiring others to find strength in times of adversity.

In the pages that follow, Bishop Dr. David E. Tompkins will lead us through life's grand tapestry, weaving together the threads of business, religion, relationships, friendships, ministry, and the unyielding spirit in brokenness. His experiences and reflections shall serve as guiding lights, illuminating our own paths as we seek purpose, understanding, and solace in a world that often defies comprehension.

Let us embark on this transformative odyssey together, walking side by side with a man whose life exemplifies the profound enigma of the Complexity Form that shapes us all. As seekers of truth, stewards of love, and believers in the resiliency of the human spirit, we shall uncover the beauty that lies within life's intricate design.

Section I: Complexity in Business – Navigating the Corporate Crossroads
How the complexity of business connects to faith.

Having a business is not easy and being a pastor with a big business can be a challenge because everything you can think of will come your way. For all of you that will pursue this route, please let me be the first to say…You better have your priorities in order, and you better have faith. My faith serves as a guiding light during challenging times in my business. It provides me with a sense of purpose and reminds me to treat all stakeholders with compassion and respect, fostering a more harmonious work environment.

Having faith allows me to maintain a positive outlook, even in the face of uncertainty. This mindset helps me navigate the complexities of my business with resilience, seeking innovative solutions and embracing change.

The principles taught by my faith encourage me to be honest and transparent in all business dealings. This approach builds trust with customers, partners, and employees, contributing to the long-term success of the company.

My faith emphasizes the importance of community and giving back. As a result, I prioritize corporate social responsibility, supporting various philanthropic initiatives and striving to make a positive impact on the world around us.

Incorporating mindfulness practices from my faith into my daily routine helps me stay grounded and focused amidst the fast-paced business environment. This allows me to make well-thought-out decisions with a clear mind.

My faith encourages continuous learning and personal growth. I apply this mindset to my business by fostering a culture of learning, encouraging my team to embrace new challenges and develop their skills.

The values instilled by my faith drive me to be environmentally conscious. Sustainability initiatives are a key aspect of our business strategy, reducing our carbon footprint and promoting eco-friendly practices.

When facing difficult decisions, I often turn to my faith for guidance. This helps me align my choices with my core beliefs, even if it means making tough sacrifices for the greater good.

My faith reminds me of the importance of empathy in leadership. Understanding the perspectives and needs of my team members enables me to be a more compassionate and effective leader. The rituals and traditions from my faith provide a sense of structure and balance in my life, helping me manage the complexities of business with a greater sense of clarity and purpose.

So, whenever you're dealing with something that is complex, like being a business owner and saving souls, you better have faith at the top of your list. Amen?

Examples of how faith has guided me

Certainly, let me share some specific examples of how my faith has played a pivotal role in guiding my business decisions. One instance that stands out is when I was faced with a challenging partnership opportunity. On the surface, it seemed financially lucrative, but I had reservations about the ethical implications of the venture. In those moments, I turned to prayer and sought guidance from my faith. Through reflection and seeking a deeper connection with God, I became more attuned to what truly mattered to me - integrity and staying true to my values.

Consequently, I decided to decline the partnership, even though it meant forgoing short-term gains. This decision turned out to be wise overall, as it strengthened the reputation of my business and solidified trust with our customers and stakeholders.

Another instance where my faith came into play was during a critical hiring process. A highly qualified candidate was being considered, but I sensed some red flags regarding their treatment of others and potential interpersonal conflicts within the team. Relying on the values taught by my faith, I chose to prioritize the importance of fostering a positive and harmonious work environment. Instead, I hired an individual with strong skills, but who also exemplified humility, respect, and a collaborative spirit. This choice not only enriched our team dynamics but also positively impacted the overall productivity and happiness of the employees.

Moreover, my faith has also influenced my approach to resolving conflicts with business partners. There was a situation where a misunderstanding with a key supplier could have escalated into a legal battle, jeopardizing both parties' interests. In this instance, I recalled the teachings of forgiveness and reconciliation from my faith. Rather than relying solely on third-party mediation or legal channels, I chose to have open and honest one-on-one discussions with the supplier. By approaching the situation with empathy and understanding, we were able to find common ground and reach a mutually beneficial resolution, preserving a valuable business relationship.

Furthermore, my faith has instilled in me the understanding that my identity and worth are not determined solely by how others treat me or by worldly success. When I faced mistreatment from certain family members, it was challenging not to let their actions define me. The two people that have always had my back have been my mother Mozelle and my dear friend Ms. Vera who has always believed in me. However, besides the two people who have been my cheerleaders, my faith reminded me that my true worth lies in my relationship with God and my commitment to living a life aligned with my spiritual beliefs. This realization empowered me to rise above negativity, focusing instead on personal growth and fostering positive relationships within both my personal and business life.

My faith is not merely a set of beliefs but a guiding force that influences every aspect of my life, including how I approach business decisions. It is in prayer, reflection, and seeking God's direction that I find clarity and wisdom to navigate the complexities of the business world, striving to make decisions that align with my core values and lead to a more purposeful and fulfilling entrepreneurial journey.

Finding connections between
my personal beliefs

Finding connections between my personal beliefs and the challenges I face as a business owner is a critical aspect of how I navigate the complexities of entrepreneurship. While I agree that rational thinking and using the brain are essential for making sound business decisions, I must also emphasize the significance of aligning my heart with my mind.

Let me explain further: my heart represents the core of my personal beliefs, the values instilled by my faith, and the ethical principles that guide my actions. By staying connected to my heart, I ensure that my decisions are not solely driven by profit or self-interest but also by a sense of purpose and responsibility towards my employees, customers, and the broader community.

However, I do recognize that the brain's logical thinking is indispensable for business success. It allows me to analyze data, assess risks, and strategize for the future. But rather than disregarding the heart, I seek a balance between emotional intelligence and analytical reasoning. When faced with tough choices, I rely on both my brain and heart. I use my brain to evaluate the practical aspects of a decision, and then I turn to my heart to assess whether it aligns with my personal beliefs and values.

Additionally, my spiritual guidance plays a crucial role in discerning the truth in various situations. It provides me with a moral compass that guides me when dealing with complex ethical dilemmas. My faith teaches me to approach these challenges with empathy, compassion, and fairness. This spiritual guidance enables me to help others in difficult situations by offering support and directing them towards resolutions that are aligned with truth and integrity.

For example, when I encounter employees or clients who may be facing personal hardships or difficult circumstances, my spiritual beliefs prompt me to extend understanding and support. I strive to create a work environment that fosters empathy and a sense of community, allowing individuals to bring their whole selves to the workplace.

Furthermore, I find that by staying true to my personal beliefs, I build trust with my team, clients, and partners. This trust forms the foundation of strong and lasting relationships, which are invaluable in the business world.

However, you do it, I believe finding connections between my personal beliefs and the challenges I face as a business owner is an ongoing and enriching journey. By integrating my heart's values with my brain's logic and seeking spiritual guidance, I aim to make decisions that not only lead to business success but maintain my integrity.

Teachings and principles vs. navigating the complexities of the business world.

The teachings and principles from my faith play a fundamental role in guiding my approach to navigating the complexities of the business world. One passage that has had a profound impact on my life is Psalm 23, which serves as a guiding light in various aspects of my business journey.

Psalm 23 speaks of the Lord as a shepherd who leads and cares for his flock. It reminds me of the importance of seeking divine guidance and wisdom in my decision-making processes. Just as a shepherd watch over and protects his sheep, I am called to be a responsible steward of my business and the well-being of all those entrusted to my care.

This scripture keeps me grounded and fosters humility in my leadership. It teaches me to acknowledge that my achievements and successes are not solely the result of my efforts but also a reflection of the support and blessings I receive from a higher power. With this humility, I approach challenges with a sense of gratitude and a willingness to learn from both successes and failures.

Additionally, Psalm 23 highlights the concept of 'walking through the valley of the shadow of death.' In the business world, we inevitably encounter tough times, obstacles, and uncertainties. However, this scripture reminds me that I need not fear these challenges, for the Lord is with me. It strengthens my resilience, enabling me to persevere through difficulties with faith and hope for a brighter outcome.

In addition to Psalm 23, there are other scriptures that have shaped my approach to business. For instance, Proverbs 16:3 reminds me to commit my plans to the Lord, trusting that He will establish them. This verse encourages me to seek divine guidance before making significant business decisions, understanding that my plans align with a higher purpose.

Another relevant teaching is found in Philippians 2:3-4, which emphasizes the importance of valuing others above oneself and looking out for their interests. This principle is vital in fostering a collaborative and harmonious work environment, encouraging teamwork, and building lasting relationships with employees, clients, and partners.

Moreover, the Sermon on the Mount in Matthew 5-7 provides valuable insights on leadership, honesty, and treating others with respect and fairness. The teachings of Jesus in these passages inspire me to embody these virtues in my daily interactions as a business owner. By integrating these teachings and principles from my faith into my business practices, I aim to create a purpose-driven, compassionate, and principled business that positively impacts the lives of all stakeholders involved.

In conclusion, my faith serves as a constant source of inspiration and guidance, offering timeless teachings and principles that inform my decision-making, leadership style, and interactions within the dynamic world of business.

Regarding employing family, friends, and members of your faith:

Employing family members, friends, and members of my faith can present both advantages and challenges in my business. Let me delve into each aspect to give you a clearer picture of my experiences.

We can learn from the Advantages:

Trust and Loyalty: One of the significant advantages is the inherent trust and loyalty that often exists among family members, friends, and those who share the same faith community. This foundation of trust can strengthen working relationships and create a supportive and unified team.

Shared Values: Employing individuals who share similar values and beliefs can lead to a more cohesive work environment. Shared values can foster a sense of purpose and common goals, aligning the team towards a collective vision.

Commitment to Success: Family members, friends, and faith community members may be more invested in the business's success because they have a personal stake in its outcomes. This heightened commitment can lead to greater dedication and a willingness to go the extra mile.

Open Communication: With familiar or like-minded individuals, communication may be more open and transparent, enabling easier resolution of conflicts and fostering a culture of collaboration.

Don't forget Life lesson from the Challenges:

Nepotism and Fairness: One of the significant challenges is navigating the perception of nepotism. If not managed properly, it may lead to dissatisfaction among other employees who feel that favoritism is at play. Ensuring fairness and meritocracy in hiring, promotions, and rewards is essential.

Separating Personal and Professional Life: Employing family and friends can blur the lines between personal and professional relationships. This may lead to difficulty in addressing performance issues or making tough decisions that could impact personal relationships.

Qualifications and Expertise: While trust is essential, it's equally crucial to ensure that family members and friends have the necessary qualifications and skills for their roles. Placing someone in a position beyond their expertise could lead to inefficiencies and hinder business growth.

Communication Challenges: Familiarity can sometimes lead to informal communication, which may not be as clear or professional as required in a business setting.

To overcome these challenges and make the most of the advantages, I have implemented specific strategies in my business. For instance, I emphasize the importance of merit-based opportunities, ensuring that family members and friends earn their positions through demonstrated skills and experience. Open and honest communication is also vital, and I encourage all employees, regardless of their relationship with me, to provide feedback and voice their concerns.

Additionally, I foster a culture of continuous learning and growth, encouraging family members and friends to pursue professional development and improve their skills. This ensures that they remain competent and valuable assets to the business.

By striking a balance between trust, professionalism, and fairness, I aim to create a workplace where family, friends, and members of my faith contribute positively to the business success while maintaining strong personal relationships outside of work.

Ensuring a balance between personal relationships and professional expectations

Maintaining a balance between personal relationships and professional expectations when working with loved ones is crucial for the success and harmony of both the business and personal life. It requires thoughtful consideration and proactive measures to establish clear boundaries and ensure a respectful working environment. Here are some specific strategies I implement to achieve this balance:

Clearly Define Roles and Expectations: Right from the outset, I ensure that roles and responsibilities for all employees, including family members and friends, are well-defined. This clarity helps avoid confusion and minimizes the risk of overlap or misunderstandings.

Professional Communication: Encouraging professional communication in the workplace is essential, regardless of personal relationships. I foster an environment where all team members, including loved ones, communicate in a manner that is respectful, constructive, and focused on the business objectives.

Separate Personal and Professional Spaces: Establishing a clear separation between personal and professional spaces is vital. I ensure that discussions related to the business occur during work hours and within the workplace, keeping personal matters for outside of work hours and locations.

Set Boundaries: To maintain a healthy balance, it's crucial to set boundaries between work and personal life. I encourage loved ones to avoid discussing work matters at family gatherings and vice versa. This way, we can cherish our personal relationships without being overly consumed by business matters.

Regular Check-ins: I regularly schedule check-in meetings with family members and friends who work in the business. During these meetings, we address any concerns, assess performance, and celebrate achievements. This formal approach helps maintain objectivity in evaluating their contributions.

Acknowledge Achievements: I think working relations improve when emphasizing the importance of recognizing and rewarding the efforts and achievements of family members and friends within the business is essential. However, I ensure that such recognition is based on merit and not solely because of personal relationships.

Emphasize Professional Development: I'm not perfect but I always try to encourage continuous learning and growth for all employees, including loved ones. By supporting their professional development, they can contribute more effectively to the business and gain a sense of personal accomplishment.

Seek External Advice: In challenging situations or decisions that involve loved ones, seeking external advice or involving a third-party mediator can provide unbiased perspectives and help resolve conflicts amicably.

Lead by Example: This is something I have been taught as a child, so as an adult and a business owner, I lead by example, demonstrating professionalism, dedication, and respect for both the business and personal aspects of life. By modeling the behavior, I expect from others, I encourage a positive work culture.

In summary, striking a balance between personal relationships and professional expectations requires proactive measures, open communication, and a commitment to maintaining a respectful and productive work environment. By implementing these strategies, I aim to nurture strong personal connections while ensuring the success and growth of the business.

Conflicts of interest vs. differing opinions

There have been instances where conflicts of interest or differing opinions arose due to employing people from my faith community. I can remember earlier in my career, when I was a used car manager (selling cars) I was so trusting. I hired anyone who needed a job and appeared honest. In trusting and believing in the honor system, I felt, it was essential to foster a sense of unity and shared values within the workplace. I also thought it was equally important to acknowledge that diverse perspectives and opinions may arise, even among individuals from the same faith background. Here are some examples of how these situations have been handled:

Differing Approaches: Individuals from my faith community may have different approaches or interpretations of how certain tasks should be carried out, which can lead to conflicts. To address this, I encourage open discussions and welcome diverse viewpoints. Through respectful dialogue, we work towards finding common ground or reaching a consensus on the best way forward.

Handling Disagreements: Disagreements can occur in any work environment, and it's no different when employing people from my faith community. When conflicts arise, I prioritize addressing the issues promptly and objectively. I promote a culture of constructive criticism, allowing employees to express their concerns and ideas without fear of reprisal.

Balancing Personal and Business Relationships: Working with individuals from my faith community sometimes involves managing dual roles—business leader and fellow community member. I ensure that I maintain a professional demeanor while also acknowledging our shared faith and personal connection. This balance helps navigate potential conflicts that may arise from overlapping relationships.

Avoiding Favoritism: To prevent perceptions of favoritism within the workplace, I am mindful of how decisions are made, and rewards are distributed. Performance and merit always guide promotions and recognition, regardless of a person's faith affiliation.

Encouraging Diversity of Thought: While employing individuals from my faith community can offer shared values, I also understand the importance of diversity of thought. I actively seek to build a team with diverse backgrounds, skills, and perspectives, which enriches the decision-making process and promotes innovation.

Implementing Conflict Resolution Strategies: In cases where conflicts persist, I leverage conflict resolution strategies, such as mediation or involving human resources, to address the issues professionally and impartially.

Fostering a Positive Work Culture: A positive work culture is essential for managing conflicts and differing opinions. I prioritize team-building activities, open communication channels, and a supportive environment that encourages collaboration and respect. In summary, while employing people from my faith community has many advantages, it also comes with the potential for conflicts and differing opinions. By proactively addressing these challenges through open communication, respectful dialogue, and a commitment to fairness, I strive to create a harmonious and inclusive work environment that benefits from the diverse perspectives of all team members.

Maintaining a fair and unbiased approach

Maintaining a fair and unbiased approach in hiring and promotions is of utmost importance to me, regardless of whether I'm working with individuals from my close circles or not. While it's natural for people to have concerns about favoritism in such situations, I want to assure you that I take proactive measures to uphold fairness and objectivity in all aspects of the hiring and promotion processes. Here's how I do it:

Clearly Defined Criteria: I establish clear and well-defined criteria for hiring and promotions, outlining the specific qualifications, skills, and experience required for each position. This ensures that all candidates are evaluated based on their merits and how well they align with the job requirements.

Anonymous Initial Review: In the initial stages of the hiring process, I anonymize resumes and applications to avoid any unconscious biases that may arise from knowing the candidate's identity or personal connection.

Diverse Hiring Panels: I assemble diverse hiring and promotion panels, comprising individuals from various backgrounds and perspectives. This diversity ensures a well-rounded evaluation and minimizes the potential for bias.

Structured Interviews: During interviews, I use a structured approach with standardized questions to ensure consistency and fairness in evaluating all candidates. This approach allows for an objective comparison of each candidate's responses.

Performance-Based Evaluations: For promotions, I base decisions on performance evaluations and demonstrated achievements. This ensures that individuals are rewarded based on their contributions and accomplishments, regardless of personal relationships.

Transparency in Decision-Making: I strive to be transparent throughout the hiring and promotion processes, providing feedback and explanations for decisions. This transparency fosters trust and understanding among all employees, including those from my close circles.

Encouraging Internal Growth: I promote a culture of continuous learning and professional development, encouraging all employees to grow within the company. This creates opportunities for deserving individuals, including those from my close circles, to advance based on their qualifications and achievements.

Addressing Concerns: I actively listen to and address any concerns or perceptions of favoritism raised by employees. Open communication allows for constructive discussions and helps dispel any misconceptions about unfair practices.

Seeking External Input: In some instances, I seek advice from external consultants or HR professionals to review and validate our hiring and promotion processes, ensuring they are unbiased and in line with best practices.

Therefore, as a pastor and entrepreneur, my commitment to maintaining a fair and unbiased approach in hiring and promotions is unwavering. I believe that fostering a diverse and inclusive workplace, coupled with transparent and structured evaluation processes, is the key to ensuring that everyone, regardless of their relationship with me, has equal opportunities to thrive and contribute to the success of the business.

Managing stress and maintaining

Managing stress and maintaining a sense of clarity amidst the complexities of running a business and managing relationships is undoubtedly essential for sustainable success and personal well-being. While it's true that pursuing something I am passionate about has brought me a sense of fulfillment, I also rely on various strategies to navigate stress and maintain focus. Here's how I approach it:

Time Management: I prioritize effective time management to balance my professional and personal life. By setting clear boundaries and allocating time for different aspects of my life, I ensure that I can devote the necessary attention to both business responsibilities and personal relationships.

Delegation: Recognizing that I can't do everything alone, I delegate tasks and responsibilities to capable team members. Delegating allows me to focus on high-priority tasks and reduces the burden of managing all aspects of the business myself.

Stress-Relief Techniques: I engage in stress-relief techniques such as meditation, mindfulness practices, and regular exercise. These activities help me clear my mind, reduce anxiety, and maintain a sense of calm amidst demanding situations.

Seeking Support: In times of stress, I don't hesitate to seek support from trusted mentors, advisors, or friends. Talking through challenges with others helps me gain fresh perspectives and valuable insights.

Continuous Learning: I believe that continuous learning is key to staying adaptable and maintaining clarity. I make time for self-development, reading industry-related materials, attending workshops, and seeking knowledge beyond my current expertise.

Constructive Conflict Resolution: Managing relationships often involves navigating conflicts. I approach conflicts with a constructive mindset, seeking resolutions that benefit all parties involved. Active listening, empathy, and effective communication are central to resolving disagreements.

Regular Reflection: I regularly set aside time for self-reflection, assessing my progress, identifying areas of improvement, and celebrating achievements. This introspective practice allows me to stay focused on my goals and maintain a sense of clarity about my business direction.

Balancing Work and Personal Life: I make it a point to take breaks, spend quality time with loved ones, and engage in hobbies and activities that bring me joy. Maintaining this balance rejuvenates me and helps prevent burnout.

Flexibility and Adaptability: In the fast-paced business world, adaptability is crucial. I remain open to change, embrace new ideas, and adjust my plans as needed to stay responsive to market dynamics and emerging opportunities.

Another thing, while pursuing my passion has undoubtedly provided a sense of purpose, managing stress, and maintaining clarity in business and relationships require deliberate efforts and a combination of strategies. By focusing on time management, self-care, seeking support, and nurturing a growth mindset, I aim to lead a fulfilling and well-balanced entrepreneurial journey.

Putting my faith to the test…

Yes, there have been moments in my entrepreneurial journey where my faith was put to the test due to complex business situations. While I have found my talent and worked through my gift, it doesn't mean that challenges haven't arisen. These moments have served as opportunities for spiritual growth and have deepened my connection with my faith. Let me share a few instances:

Overcoming Financial Struggles: Early on in my business venture, I faced significant financial challenges. There were times when it seemed impossible to keep the business afloat. During these moments of uncertainty, my faith became a source of strength and hope. I relied on prayer and trust in a higher power to guide me through difficult financial decisions and to remain steadfast in my determination to pursue my entrepreneurial dreams.

Navigating Ethical Dilemmas: As a business owner, I've encountered ethical dilemmas where the choices weren't black and white. These situations put my values to the test. My faith taught me the importance of honesty, integrity, and compassion. Turning to my spiritual beliefs, I sought wisdom and discernment in making decisions that aligned with my conscience and upheld my core principles.

Dealing with Unexpected Losses: In business, unforeseen losses or setbacks can be disheartening.

There were times when I experienced disappointments, such as failed partnerships or losing a key client. My faith provided solace during these moments of disappointment, reminding me to remain resilient and keep moving forward with hope and determination.

Balancing Priorities: Running a business can be all-consuming, and at times, it has challenged my ability to balance personal life and work responsibilities. My faith encourages me to prioritize family, self-care, and community involvement. It's a constant effort to strike the right balance, and my faith serves as a guiding force in making these decisions.

Trusting the Journey: Entrepreneurship is filled with uncertainties and risks. There were moments when doubt crept in, questioning whether I was on the right path. During these times of self-doubt, my faith provided a sense of reassurance that I am on the journey I was meant to be on, and that challenges are a part of growth and learning.

Fostering Forgiveness: In the realm of business, disagreements and conflicts can arise. My faith has taught me the importance of forgiveness and reconciliation. It has helped me approach conflicts with compassion, seeking resolutions that promote understanding and healing.

While I have found my talent and worked through my gift, my faith has been tested in various complex business situations. Each challenge has been an opportunity for personal and spiritual growth, and my faith has been a source of strength and guidance. Embracing the lessons learned from these experiences, I continue to navigate the complexities of entrepreneurship with a deep-rooted sense of purpose and faith.

Finding meaning and purpose in your work…

Finding meaning and purpose in my work is at the core of my entrepreneurial journey, especially when faced with the inevitable challenges that come my way.

I believe that true fulfillment comes from a combination of factors that align with my passion, values, and the impact I have on others. I believe this formula can work for you too! Here's how I find meaning and purpose in my work while navigating challenges:

Impactful Problem-Solving: I experience genuine joy in tackling complex problems and finding innovative solutions. Each challenge that arises becomes an opportunity to apply my skills and knowledge to create positive outcomes. The satisfaction of overcoming obstacles and contributing to the success of my business and those I serve brings immense meaning to my work.

Focusing on the Bigger Picture: While challenges can be daunting, I remind myself of the greater purpose behind my work. By focusing on the positive impact my business has on customers, employees, and the community, I find motivation and a sense of purpose that drives me forward, even during challenging times.

Not Taking Situations Personally: I approach challenges with a level-headed and objective perspective. Instead of internalizing setbacks or viewing them as personal failures, I look at each situation as an opportunity to learn and grow. This mindset helps me maintain clarity and resilience while addressing the challenges that come my way.

Exceptional Problem-Solving: Each challenge presents a unique set of circumstances, requiring an exceptional approach. By embracing the uniqueness of every situation, I am inspired to think creatively and outside the box. This commitment to finding exceptional solutions enhances my sense of purpose in serving my business and its stakeholders.

Making a Difference: My work extends beyond mere profit-making; it is about making a positive difference in the lives of others. Whether it's providing products or services that improve people's lives or creating job opportunities for my team members, knowing that my work has a tangible impact brings immense fulfillment.

Cultivating a Positive Work Environment: As a business leader, I recognize the influence I have on my team's well-being and growth. I find meaning in fostering a positive work environment that promotes collaboration, professional development, and a sense of belonging among my employees.

Embracing Continuous Growth: Challenges are opportunities for personal growth, and I embrace each hurdle as a chance to refine my skills, deepen my expertise, and expand my knowledge. This commitment to continuous growth enhances my sense of purpose in pursuing my entrepreneurial journey.

In conclusion, finding meaning and purpose in my work while dealing with challenges is an ongoing process of embracing joy in problem-solving, maintaining a clear perspective, and understanding the positive impact I have on others. By cultivating a growth-oriented mindset and focusing on the greater purpose of my business, I am driven to overcome challenges and stay aligned with my sense of purpose throughout my entrepreneurial endeavors. I recommend that you try this approach and see what happens!

Discovering innovative solutions…

My faith has been a guiding force in discovering innovative solutions and approaches to handle complex business issues. The values and principles instilled by my faith have had a profound impact on my leadership style and decision-making. Let me share some specific examples of how my faith has influenced my approach to problem-solving:

Embracing Patience and Calmness: In the face of challenges and uncertainties, my faith encourages me to remain patient and calm. Rather than hastily reacting to issues, I take the time to understand the root causes and underlying dynamics. This patient approach allows me to see the bigger picture and explore various possibilities before making decisions.

Seeking Balance: My faith emphasizes the importance of seeking balance in all aspects of life, including business. I strive to strike a balance between short-term objectives and long-term vision. This holistic approach enables me to address immediate challenges while keeping the business's overall purpose and sustainability in mind.

Nurturing a Supportive Work Culture: My faith teaches me the value of compassion, empathy, and understanding. I apply these principles in nurturing a supportive work culture where team members feel valued, heard, and encouraged to contribute their unique perspectives. This inclusivity fosters an environment where innovative ideas are freely shared and cultivated.

Drawing Inspiration from Adversity: Adversity often brings valuable lessons and opportunities for growth. My faith has taught me to draw inspiration from challenging experiences and view them as opportunities for learning and transformation. This mindset encourages me to approach complex business issues with resilience and a willingness to explore unconventional solutions.

Integrating Ethical Considerations: Ethical decision-making is a cornerstone of my business practices, influenced by my faith's teachings. When confronted with complex issues, I prioritize ethical considerations and ensure that my decisions align with my values and the greater good of all stakeholders involved.

Trusting Divine Guidance: My faith has instilled in me a sense of trust in divine guidance. While I rely on my skills, knowledge, and experience, I also recognize the importance of seeking spiritual wisdom during critical decision-making moments. This spiritual guidance has often led me to innovative solutions and provided clarity when facing difficult choices.

Emphasizing Collaboration: In complex business issues, I encourage collaboration and teamwork. By fostering an environment of open communication and collective problem-solving, I harness the diverse expertise and insights of my team. This collaborative approach often leads to innovative and comprehensive solutions.

In conclusion, my faith serves as a wellspring of inspiration and guidance in handling complex business issues. By remaining grounded, patient, and calm, and drawing on the ethical principles and values instilled by my faith, I find innovative solutions that address challenges while aligning with my sense of purpose and the well-being of all involved.

Supporting Sciptures for Section 1

Here are some scriptures that will support this section on complexities in business:

The Bible provides wisdom and guidance that can be applied to the complexities of business and navigating the corporate crossroads. Here are a few scriptures that highlight principles relevant to this aspect of life:

Proverbs 16:3 (NIV) "Commit to the Lord whatever you do, and he will establish your plans." This verse reminds us of the importance of seeking God's guidance and wisdom in all our endeavors, including business. By committing our plans to Him, we acknowledge His sovereignty over our lives and invite His direction in navigating the complexities of the corporate world.

Proverbs 22:29 (NIV) "Do you see someone skilled in their work? They will serve before kings; they will not serve before officials of low rank."
This verse emphasizes the value of skill and excellence in business. When we approach our work with diligence and excellence, we position ourselves for success and the opportunity to impact influential individuals in the corporate sphere.

Matthew 6:33 (NIV) "But seek first his kingdom and his righteousness, and all these things will be given to you as well."

In the pursuit of business goals, it's essential to maintain a priority of seeking God's kingdom and righteousness. Aligning our actions with God's principles helps us navigate the complexities of business with integrity and purpose.

Colossians 3:23-24 (NIV) "Whatever you do, work at it with all your heart, as working for the Lord, not for human masters since you know that you will receive an inheritance from the Lord as a reward. It is the Lord Christ you are serving."

This scripture underscores the significance of approaching business with a heart of service to God. When we recognize that our work is an act of worship, we are motivated to navigate the corporate crossroads with diligence, honesty, and a commitment to honoring God in all we do.

Proverbs 11:1 (NIV) "The Lord detests dishonest scales, but accurate weights find favor with him."

Integrity and honesty are vital in business dealings. This verse reminds us that dishonest practices are displeasing to God, and ethical conduct should be the foundation upon which we navigate the complexities of business.

Luke 16:10 (NIV) "Whoever can be trusted with very little can also be trusted with much, and whoever is dishonest with very little will also be dishonest with much."

This verse speaks to the importance of integrity and trustworthiness in business. How we handle small matters can reflect our character and readiness for greater responsibilities. Navigating the corporate crossroads involves demonstrating faithfulness in all aspects of our work.

Remember, these scriptures provide guidance and principles that can be applied to the complexity of business. By seeking God's wisdom and following His precepts, we can navigate the corporate world with integrity, purpose, and a commitment to serve Him in all that we do.

Section II: Complexity in Religion – Faith Woven in Time

In this chapter, we delve deeper into the intricate tapestry of Bishop Tompkins' faith, exploring the threads that have woven his spiritual journey throughout the annals of religious history. We uncover how his unwavering belief in sacred scriptures and divine guidance has served as a wellspring of solace and inspiration, shaping his perspectives on profound matters of morality, justice, and compassion.

At the core of Bishop Tompkins' life story lies a foundation of faith that took root in his early years. Growing up in a community deeply steeped in religious tradition, he was exposed to the teachings and rituals that had endured through generations. It was during these formative years that the seeds of faith were sown, sowing the path that would lead him to become a prominent servant of God.

Morality, a fundamental pillar of faith, is intricately woven into Bishop Tompkins' worldview. We explore how his faith instills a sense of responsibility to live according to the moral principles and values outlined in his religious teachings. His perspectives on right and wrong are not only personal convictions but also the underpinning of his role as a spiritual leader guiding others along the path of righteousness.

As we journey through the annals of Bishop Tompkins' religious history, we uncover how his faith has influenced his understanding of justice. Beyond mere legal systems, justice becomes a divine calling that transcends societal norms. We learn how he grapples with the complexities of seeking justice in an imperfect world and how his faith drives him to be an advocate for the oppressed and marginalized.

Compassion, like a thread woven throughout Bishop Tompkins' life, shapes his interactions with the world around him. We explore how his faith calls him to embody compassion in his daily life, reaching out to those in need and fostering a sense of empathy for all beings. His reflections on compassion offer profound insights into the heart of a servant of God who seeks to alleviate suffering and spread love in a troubled world.

Even as Bishop Tompkins' faith has provided him with solace and guidance, we acknowledge that it is not without its complexities. We examine the challenges he faces as a spiritual leader and how the diversity of interpretations within his community can lead to moments of doubt and introspection. His honest reflections reveal the delicate balance between staying steadfast in faith and embracing the diversity of human perspectives.

As we journey deeper into the heart of faith with Bishop Tompkins, readers will witness the transformation of a young believer into a profound spiritual leader. Each step of his journey will be an exploration of the rich tapestry of faith woven through time, guiding him as a servant of God, and inspiring others to seek their own connections to the divine in the complexities of life.

Pivotal moments or experiences in my life…

As one of my favorite songstress Ms. Patti LaBelle says in a song, "If you ask me to, I just might change my mind and let you in my heart forever." For you that know me, my deep sense of faith and connection to my religious beliefs were shaped by pivotal moments and experiences earlier in life where God has led me to change my mind based on tolerance. It's easy for me to acknowledge the faith that I believes God has bestowed upon me tolerance and because of that I believe that my strongest moments emerged from life's challenges. I have been able to draw strength from negative experiences, using them as opportunities for growth, and consistently upholding my faith, avoiding any tendencies to exaggerate or falsely claim spiritual experiences.

My faith holds immense value in my life. As I recall an important message from my mother, who foresaw a positive and distinctive path for me, instilled in me a desire to acquire counseling skills and to genuinely listen to people. Over time, this aspiration led me to a calling in preaching.

However, my journey towards a profound faith and connection to my religious beliefs was influenced by significant life experiences, my unwavering trust in God, and the guidance of my mother's foresight, all of which directed me toward the current path of preaching and helping others through counseling.

Interpreting and understanding...

When it comes to interpreting and understanding the sacred scriptures of my faith, I follow a thoughtful approach. My aim is to share both my theoretical insights and personal experiences related to the gospel. In this endeavor, I hold a strong belief that every word within the scriptures carries meaning and significance.

Therefore, I invest considerable effort in comprehending the scriptures thoroughly, striving to extract their wisdom and relevance.

This process of interpretation isn't merely an academic exercise for me; it deeply affects my daily life and interactions. I take the teachings and principles I glean from the scriptures and apply them to my own experiences and circumstances. This practice not only shapes my personal moral compass but also influences the way I deliver my sermons and engage with my community.

In essence, my interpretation of the sacred scriptures is a dynamic journey of understanding, connection, and application. It is a process that continually enriches my perspective on right and wrong, guiding me in living a more meaningful and purposeful life.

*Faith guided, but difficult moral
decision/ethical dilemma*

Instances where my faith has played a pivotal role in guiding me through challenging moral decisions are quite common in my daily life. Allow me to share a couple of specific situations to shed light on how this process unfolds:

One example that stands out is when I face a professional dilemma. I had the choice to compromise on a fundamental principle in order to achieve a short-term gain. However, my faith rooted me firmly in the belief that integrity and honesty should never be sacrificed for immediate success. This conviction guided me to opt for the ethically sound route, even though it meant potentially forgoing certain benefits.

Another instance involves a personal relationship that had taken a strained turn. The temptation to respond with anger and resentment was strong, but my faith reminded me of the importance of forgiveness and empathy. Drawing from my religious teachings, I chose to approach the situation with understanding and compassion, fostering a path toward healing and resolution.

These examples underscore how my faith serves as a compass, steering me towards choices aligned with my core values, even in the face of challenging ethical dilemmas. Each day presents opportunities to exercise this guidance, reaffirming my commitment to a principled life.

Faith vs. social issues and advocacy

In my role as a servant of God, my approach to the concept of justice is rooted in a balanced perspective, one that combines thoughtful reasoning with compassionate action. It's important to emphasize that I believe in making decisions based on both rationality and empathy. While my faith serves as a guiding light, I also acknowledge the significance of using sound judgment to navigate complex situations.

Regarding social issues and advocacy for those in need, my faith has played a profound role in shaping my stance. I view success not as a shield from the world's challenges, but rather as an avenue to hear and address the heart-wrenching stories that often go unheard. It's true that many seek quick fixes, but I firmly believe that genuine solutions require dedicated effort and a willingness to confront difficult realities.

My enduring concern lies in understanding the root causes that lead individuals into various situations. This awareness fuels my commitment to actively engage with social issues, seeking to contribute to meaningful change. As a spiritual leader, I am deeply committed to living in alignment with the teachings of Jesus. This includes modeling a lifestyle that reflects his values of compassion, empathy, and justice.

By embodying these principles, I aim to approach social issues with a sense of responsibility and wisdom. This entails addressing them not only with empathy but also with the intention of fostering lasting transformation.

My faith, therefore, serves as a compass that guides me toward thoughtful action, enabling me to navigate the complexities of social issues while upholding the teachings I hold dear.

Compassion anyone?

Let's talk about compassion. Compassion holds a significant place within my daily life and interactions with others, particularly within the context of my role as a spiritual leader. It's crucial to strike a balance in how compassion is expressed and applied. Allow me to elaborate on this principle:

Compassion forms the foundation of my approach to guiding and supporting individuals. I believe in genuinely caring for the well-being of those I serve, understanding their challenges, and empathizing with their struggles. This compassionate stance allows for a deep connection and a safe space where individuals can share their burdens. I have helped many people based on the love I have for myself and the compassion I have for people in general, plus, the people I center around me in the pulpit and at my job are on the same page with me when it comes to compassion.

However, it's essential to recognize that compassion alone might not always lead to lasting solutions. While offering empathy and understanding, I am also acutely aware of the potential pitfalls of enabling dependency or failing to address underlying issues. Compassion should not inadvertently contribute to perpetuating problems at church, at home, in the community or on the job.

In my experience, compassion should be coupled with a commitment to empowering and uplifting individuals. This involves providing the necessary tools, resources, and education to help them overcome their challenges and find sustainable solutions. While compassion opens the door, practical assistance and guidance are crucial steps in guiding individuals towards healing and growth.

In essence, compassion, when properly channeled, can be a powerful force for positive change. It enriches the human connection, encourages vulnerability, and fosters an environment where individuals can thrive. However, it must always be complemented by a proactive and educational approach that aims to address the root causes of issues and equip individuals with the means to overcome them. This comprehensive strategy ensures that compassion is a catalyst for meaningful transformation rather than a potential hindrance.

The church's' challenges vs. navigating faith with a diversified community

In our journey of guiding our community towards salvation, we have encountered several significant challenges that arise from the diversity of perspectives within our congregation. One of the foremost challenges is the varying interpretations of religious teachings and beliefs. People come from different backgrounds, cultures, and life experiences, which can lead to differing understandings of scripture and spiritual practices.

Another challenge we frequently encounter is the need to balance traditional teachings with evolving societal norms. As the world changes, questions arise about how certain teachings should be applied in contemporary contexts. This requires us to engage in thoughtful discussions and discernment to ensure that our faith remains relevant and inclusive.

Moreover, the issue of inclusivity itself poses a challenge. We aim to create a welcoming and accepting space for all individuals, regardless of their backgrounds or beliefs. However, finding common ground and fostering understanding among diverse viewpoints can sometimes be daunting.

Navigating these challenges has taught us the importance of self-control and empathy. We've learned to listen actively and engage in open dialogue, allowing us to appreciate the various perspectives that enrich our community. It's also crucial to approach these conversations with a willingness to learn from one another, as well as to adapt our approaches to better resonate with the evolving needs of our congregation.

Through these experiences, we've realized that the journey of faith is not a solitary path but a collective endeavor. We continually seek ways to bridge differences, promote unity, and deepen our understanding of God's teachings. While challenges persist, they also provide us with opportunities to strengthen our bonds as a community of believers, fostering an environment where everyone can grow spiritually and find a shared sense of purpose.

Moments of doubt as a spiritual leader?

Throughout my faith journey, I have been fortunate not to experience moments of doubt in the core beliefs that guide my spirituality. My unwavering faith in divine purpose and teachings has provided a solid foundation for my role as a spiritual leader. However, like any human being, I have encountered moments of reflection and contemplation, where I've questioned the path, I've chosen.

In these moments, I have sought solace in prayer, meditation, and deep study of sacred texts. I believe that questioning and seeking deeper understanding is a natural part of spiritual growth. It allows me to explore the intricacies of my faith and emerge with a stronger, more nuanced perspective.

Reconciling these moments of reflection with my role as a spiritual leader has been an enlightening journey. I recognize that my position comes with the responsibility to guide and support others on their paths of faith. While I may have personal moments of introspection, I understand that my role extends beyond my individual experiences.

To navigate these challenges, I've found it essential to foster a sense of community and open dialogue within our congregation. I encourage open discussions about doubts and questions, creating an environment where individuals feel safe to express their uncertainties. This not only allows for collective learning but also reinforces the idea that doubt can be a catalyst for deeper faith.

Additionally, I remind myself that being a spiritual leader doesn't require having all the answers. It's about providing guidance, empathy, and a listening ear to those who seek it. By acknowledging my own moments of questioning, I hope to connect with others on a more profound level and show that faith is a journey we all undertake together.

My journey has taught me that moments of doubt or questioning are not a sign of weakness but an opportunity for growth. They remind me of the humility that comes with being a spiritual leader and the importance of continuously nurturing my own spiritual well-being while serving the needs of my community.

Faith has provided solace and inspiration during difficult times…

One profound experience that comes to mind is when I faced a particularly challenging period in my career. While my job was going well, there were still moments of uncertainty and setbacks that left me questioning my path. During these times, my faith acted as a constant pillar of support. It provided me with a sense of purpose and reminded me that every challenge I encountered was an opportunity for growth. Through prayer and reflection, I found the strength to persevere, make important decisions, and navigate through those difficult professional times.

Moreover, one of the most impactful instances of how faith has come to the aid of our South Carolina community and around the globe was during a crisis that affected many families due to two (Hurricane Hugo and COVID-19) natural disasters. Our communities were devastated, homes were destroyed, and people were grappling with immense loss. During this chaos, our faith congregation rallied together, providing not just material support but also a deep sense of spiritual comfort. We organized prayer vigils, support groups, and outreach initiatives to help those in need. Witnessing the resilience and compassion of our community members, fueled by their faith, was truly inspiring. It was a testament to the power of unity and the unwavering strength that faith can bring in times of adversity.

Furthermore, I recall a personal moment of crisis when a marriage ended in a less fortunate manner. It was a profoundly difficult period in my life, filled with emotional turmoil and uncertainty about the future. During this time, my faith served as an anchor, guiding me towards healing and acceptance. Prayer and self-reflection allowed me to find inner peace and to focus on personal growth. It was through this experience that I gained a deeper understanding of the importance of empathy, compassion, and forgiveness – values that continue to shape my role as a spiritual leader.

In sharing these stories, my aim is to underline the remarkable ways in which faith has been a source of solace, strength, and inspiration. These experiences have reinforced my belief that, even in the darkest of times, our faith has the power to light our way and lead us towards renewal, both individually and as a community.

Striking a balance in the South...

Whether you're in the south or the north, maintaining a balance between upholding the principles of my faith and respecting the diverse beliefs and perspectives of others is a fundamental aspect of my role as a religious leader. While founding and leading the church has afforded me a unique perspective, it's crucial to emphasize that this responsibility comes with a profound commitment to inclusivity and understanding.

One of the most rewarding aspects of my journey has been establishing the church and its guiding principles. This foundation allows me to create an environment where the teachings and values I hold dear can be nurtured and shared with the congregation. However, this doesn't imply an imposition of my beliefs onto others. Instead, it serves as a framework for fostering spiritual growth and community development.

In interacting with individuals who hold differing beliefs, my approach centers around empathy, active listening, and open dialogue. I believe that respectful engagement with diverse perspectives enriches our collective understanding and strengthens our unity. Rather than approaching differences as obstacles, I view them as opportunities for mutual learning and growth.

To strike this balance effectively, I encourage an atmosphere of respect and mutual appreciation within the congregation. We engage in thoughtful discussions, study sessions, and community events that allow for a genuine exchange of ideas. This approach enables us to honor our faith's principles while also acknowledging the validity of diverse viewpoints.

Furthermore, as a leader, I see it as my duty to promote a sense of shared humanity. By focusing on our common values and aspirations, we can find common ground and build bridges of understanding. This extends beyond the walls of our church and into the broader community, where collaboration and cooperation become essential tools for positive change.

My role as a founder and head of the church has empowered me to set a tone of inclusivity and respect, but it's important to note that this isn't about rigid control. It's about fostering an environment where the principles we hold dear can coexist harmoniously with the beliefs of others. Through continuous dialogue, mutual respect, and a commitment to our shared humanity, I strive to navigate the intricate balance between upholding my faith's principles and embracing the diverse perspectives that enrich our spiritual journey.

On a spiritual journey?

If you're on a spiritual journey, building a strong connection with your faith and finding guidance is a deeply personal and rewarding endeavor. In addition to being real and true to yourself, here are a few more pieces of advice that I believe can help you along your path:

Embrace Humility and Openness: Remember that none of us has all the answers. Approach your spiritual journey with humility, acknowledging that there is always more to learn and explore. Stay open to new ideas, perspectives, and insights, as they can enrich your understanding and lead to profound growth.

Seek Knowledge and Understanding: Study and delve into the teachings, scriptures, and texts of your faith. Seek out opportunities for learning, whether through books, classes, lectures, or discussions. A deeper understanding of the foundations of your faith can provide a solid grounding for your journey.

Practice Self-Reflection: Regularly take time for self-reflection and introspection. Consider your values, beliefs, and experiences, and how they align with your faith. This self-awareness can help you identify areas for growth and guide your actions in accordance with your spiritual principles.

Engage in Prayer and Meditation: Cultivate a practice of prayer and meditation that resonates with you. These practices can provide moments of connection, stillness, and clarity, allowing you to deepen your relationship with the divine and gain insight into your spiritual path.

Connect with Community: Engage with a supportive community of fellow seekers or members of your faith. Sharing experiences, insights, and challenges with others can offer a sense of belonging and provide valuable perspectives on your journey.

Practice Compassion and Service: Live out your faith through acts of compassion and service to others.

Engaging in acts of kindness and helping those in need can be a powerful way to align your actions with your spiritual beliefs.

Navigate Challenges with Resilience: Understand that challenges and moments of doubt are a natural part of any journey of faith. Instead of being discouraged by them, view them as opportunities for growth. Embrace these challenges as catalysts for deepening your understanding and commitment.

Cultivate Gratitude: Develop a practice of gratitude to foster a positive mindset. Recognize and appreciate the blessings, lessons, and moments of connection that come from your spiritual journey.

Stay Patient and Persistent: Deepening your faith is a lifelong process that requires patience and persistence. Be gentle with yourself and remember that growth takes time. Celebrate your progress and the small victories along the way.

Seek Guidance from Spiritual Leaders: Don't hesitate to seek guidance from knowledgeable and experienced spiritual leaders within your faith community. Their insights and wisdom can offer valuable direction and support as you navigate your journey.

Remember, your spiritual journey is unique to you. It's about fostering a meaningful connection with your faith, developing a deeper understanding of yourself, and aligning your actions with your spiritual principles. By integrating these pieces of advice into your journey, you can embark on a path of profound growth, self-discovery, and spiritual fulfillment.

Faith and spirituality can play a role in fostering understanding, tolerance, and unity..

Promoting understanding and unity in a diverse and divided world is a profound task that faith and spirituality can address in transformative ways. While acknowledging the role of accepting and dealing with brokenness within the congregation, there are several key aspects to consider:

Embrace Diversity as a Divine Creation: Recognize that diversity reflects the divine creation. Inherent within many faith traditions is the idea that all individuals are created equal and valued by a higher power. This recognition can serve as a foundation for treating one another with respect and fostering unity despite our differences.

Practice Empathy and Compassion: Central to many spiritual teachings is the principle of empathy and compassion. By understanding and sharing in the joys and struggles of others, we can bridge divides and develop a deeper appreciation for the unique journeys of those around us.

Engage in Open Dialogue: Faith communities can serve as safe spaces for open dialogue where individuals from various backgrounds can come together to discuss their perspectives, beliefs, and concerns.

Promote Shared Values: Identify and promote shared values that transcend differences. Many faith traditions emphasize principles such as love, justice, and kindness. By focusing on these shared values, we can build connections and foster a sense of unity that transcends cultural or ideological divisions.

Encourage Education and Awareness: Provide opportunities for education and awareness about different cultures, beliefs, and traditions. This can help dispel stereotypes, promote understanding, and create a more inclusive environment.

Social Justice and Inequality: Many faiths call for social justice and addressing inequality. By working collectively to tackle social issues and promote equality, faith communities can set an example of how unity can lead to positive change.

Lead by Example: Faith leaders can demonstrate unity by collaborating across denominations and faiths to address familiar challenges, thereby showing the broader community the power of coming together.

Celebrate Diversity: Organize events and activities that celebrate diversity within the community. This can include cultural festivals, interfaith gatherings, and collaborative projects that highlight the richness of diverse backgrounds.

Promote Forgiveness and Reconciliation: Encourage practices of forgiveness and reconciliation, which can help heal wounds and mend relationships, contributing to a more harmonious and united community.

Extend Outreach Beyond the Congregation: Extend acts of kindness, service, and support beyond the walls of the congregation to include the wider community. By embodying the values of faith in action, you can inspire others to join in creating a more understanding and united world.

The journey toward fostering understanding, tolerance, and unity in a diverse world requires a commitment to practicing the principles of faith and spirituality in tangible ways. By cultivating empathy, promoting dialogue, and embracing shared values, faith communities can serve as beacons of hope, demonstrating that despite the brokenness we encounter, a collective effort can bridge divides and create a more inclusive and harmonious society.

Envisioning the future of my community

Envisioning the future of our community is a dynamic process, one that involves a proactive and inclusive approach to engaging with the needs and aspirations of the people we serve. As a religious leader, I am committed to ensuring that the role of religion goes beyond the confines of traditional Sunday services, extending into meaningful and impactful connections with our community members.

In this vision, I see our church as a hub of not only spiritual growth but also practical empowerment. We are moving towards a direction where we actively invite community members into workshops and initiatives that address their specific needs and challenges. These workshops might encompass a wide range of topics, from financial literacy and job readiness to mental health support and family counseling. By tailoring our offerings to meet these needs, we aim to provide tangible assistance that uplifts individuals and families in our community.

Crucially, I believe that for the church to be a positive force, it must actively engage with and be embedded in the community it serves. This means collaborating with local organizations, schools, and businesses to create a holistic approach to community development. By doing so, we ensure that our efforts align with the broader goals and initiatives of our neighborhood, amplifying the positive impact we can have collectively.

Our church's mission is to be a beacon of hope and compassion, not only within our walls but also throughout the entirety of our community. This vision requires us to be attentive listeners, continuously seeking feedback from community members to ensure that our initiatives are relevant and effective.

As we move forward, I envision a community where the church stands as a trusted partner, a source of support, and a catalyst for positive change. By prioritizing the upliftment of our community and actively addressing its needs, we can demonstrate the transformative potential of religion in shaping a more inclusive, empowered, and harmonious future.

Supporting Sciptures for Section 1I

The Bible contains numerous scriptures that highlight the complexities of faith and its timeless significance. Here are some verses that underscore the intricate nature of religion and faith:

Hebrews 11:1 (NIV) "Now faith is confidence in what we hope for and assurance about what we do not see.

This foundational verse defines faith and captures its complexity. Faith involves trust in the unseen, the intangible, and the divine. It is the bedrock upon which religion is built, guiding believers through the complexities of life's journey.

Isaiah 55:8-9 (NIV) "For my thoughts are not your thoughts, neither are your ways my ways," declares the Lord. "As the heavens are higher than the earth, so are my ways higher than your ways and my thoughts than your thoughts."

These verses remind us of the profound mystery of God and His divine plan. Religion often grapples with the enigmatic nature of the divine, inviting believers to embrace humility and awe in the face of the complexities of God's ways.

Romans 11:33 (NIV) "Oh, the depth of the riches of the wisdom and knowledge of God! How unsearchable his judgments, and his paths beyond tracing out!"

This verse marvels at the unfathomable wisdom and knowledge of God. Religion acknowledges that divine understanding goes beyond human comprehension, emphasizing the depth and complexity of the spiritual realm.

Proverbs 3:5-6 (NIV) "Trust in the Lord with all your heart and lean not on your own understanding; in all your ways submit to him, and he will make your paths straight."

In the complexities of religion, believers are encouraged to place their trust in God and submit to His guidance. It reminds us that faith involves surrendering our limited understanding and relying on God's wisdom to navigate the intricate paths of life.

1 Corinthians 2:10 (NIV) "These are the things God has revealed to us by his Spirit. The Spirit searches all things, even the deep things of God."

This verse speaks to the revelation of divine truths through the Holy Spirit. Complexity in religion is met with spiritual discernment and understanding, revealing deeper insights into God's nature and purpose.

Ecclesiastes 3:11 (NIV) "He has made everything beautiful in its time. He has also set eternity in the human heart; yet no one can fathom what God has done from beginning to end."

This verse acknowledges the beauty and mystery of God's plan, which is intricately woven throughout time. The human heart yearns for the eternal, yet the complexity of God's work transcends human comprehension.

These scriptures reflect the intricate nature of faith and its profound role in religion. They remind us that, while the complexities of faith may be beyond our complete understanding, they are an integral part of our journey in seeking a deeper connection with the divine. Through trust, humility, and reliance on God's wisdom, we embrace the timeless significance of faith, intricately woven in the fabric of human existence.

Section III: Complexity in Relationships and Friendships - Threads of Love and Trust

Central to Dr. Tompkins' ministry was a profound appreciation for the intricate threads of love and trust that bind humanity together. In this chapter, we will delve into the depths of relationships and friendships, uncovering the transformative power of empathy, forgiveness, and unconditional love. Through personal anecdotes and pastoral experiences, we will discover how he nurtured profound connections and how he helped others mend the broken pieces of their relationships.

Complexity in Relationships and Friendships - Threads of Love and Trust

At the heart of Dr. Tompkins' ministry lies a deep appreciation for the intricacies of human connection. Through the highs and lows of relationships and friendships, he unveils the power of love, forgiveness, and empathy in fostering profound bonds that transcend the passage of time.

Placing emphasis where emphasis is due…

Dr. Tompkins' ministry is firmly rooted in a profound comprehension of the complexities intrinsic to human entwinements. Throughout the undulating crests and troughs of relationships and friendships, he masterfully exposes the formidable prowess harbored by love, forgiveness, and empathy, acting as catalysts for the germination of profound ties that stand impervious to the erosions of time.

When Dr. Tompkins was inquired about specific instances within his ministry where he vested importance in human connections, he alluded to Mark 1:9-11, wherein he emphasized the necessity of relinquishing detrimental influences to be repositories of love, forgiveness, and empathy within our companionship circles. How might Bishop Tompkins articulate this sentiment with heightened precision?

Reflecting upon my ministry's focal tenets, one finds a deep-seated veneration for the threads intricately knitting together the very fabric of human rapport. As we navigate through the undulating tapestry of relationships and friendships, we unearth an extraordinary triumvirate: love, forgiveness, and empathy, each possessing an unparalleled transformative potential that propels us beyond the constraints of temporal boundaries.

In response to the query concerning instances that underscore my dedication to human connections, I draw upon the wisdom encapsulated in Mark 1:9-11. This passage invites contemplation on the necessity of relinquishing detrimental influences, permitting us to channel love, forgiveness, and empathy within our relational spheres. By allowing these virtuous essences to illuminate our interactions, we pave the way for bonds that not only endure but flourish, standing resilient against the erosive forces of time.

In Dr. Tompkins' exposition of Mark 1:9-11, he draws a significant parallel between the spiritual message embedded in the scripture and the principles he adhered to in fostering meaningful human connections. In this passage, which narrates the baptism of Jesus by John the Baptist, Bishop Tompkins identifies a profound lesson that resonates with his emphasis on love, forgiveness, and empathy as foundational elements in relationships and friendships.

Mark 1:9-11 recounts the moment when Jesus is baptized by John in the Jordan River, and as he emerges from the water, the heavens open, and the Spirit descends like a dove, while a voice from heaven proclaims Jesus as the beloved Son in whom God is well pleased.

Dr. Tompkins' interpretation of this passage aligns with his ministry's core values:

Letting Go of the Wrong Spirit: Just as Jesus emerged from the waters, symbolizing a new beginning, Bishop

Tompkins urges us to shed negativity and detrimental influences from our lives. This process of spiritual cleansing parallels the act of releasing negative energies or harmful relationships that can hinder the cultivation of love, forgiveness, and empathy.

Receiving Divine Love and Approval: The voice from heaven declaring Jesus as the beloved Son reflects the idea of being affirmed and loved unconditionally. Dr. Tompkins' ministry emphasizes the power of unconditional love as a foundational element in human relationships. By acknowledging our inherent worth and extending the same affirmation to others, we create an environment conducive to authentic connections.

Empathy and Connection: The descent of the Spirit like a dove signifies the embodiment of a gentle and compassionate presence. Dr. Tompkins' focus on empathy aligns with this symbolism, as empathy allows us to understand and connect with others on a deeper level, fostering bonds that transcend superficiality.

Forgiveness and Transformation: The act of baptism itself is often associated with spiritual purification and rebirth. In the context of Dr. Tompkins' message, this can symbolize the transformative power of forgiveness. Just as Jesus' baptism marked a pivotal moment in his journey, extending forgiveness can lead to the mending and transformation of fractured relationships.

By intertwining the themes of spiritual renewal, love, forgiveness, empathy, and affirmation from Mark 1:9-11, Dr. Tompkins illustrates how these biblical principles underpin his approach to nurturing meaningful connections among people.

Defining the concept of love

When defining and discussing the concept of love within the concept of my ministry, I refer to the book of Mark, where a pivotal narrative is found in the passages that describe the baptism of Jesus. This event unveils a profound truth about the nature of love and its correlation with the spirits that surround us. Just as

Jesus emerged from the waters of baptism, divested of any detrimental influences, we too can experience the purity of love when we rid ourselves of negative energies and harmful influences. I have preached this sermon several times.

By aligning our lives with the spirit of love, as exemplified by Jesus' transformative experience, we create an environment where love can flourish effortlessly. The act of letting go of certain spirits, as referred to in the context of Mark, refers to distancing ourselves from attitudes, behaviors, and relationships that impede the free flow of genuine love.

My ministry underscores that the essence of love becomes clear and attainable when we consciously choose to surround ourselves with positive influences, shedding those spirits that hinder its expression. By doing so, we lay the groundwork for profound connections, authentic relationships, and a nurturing atmosphere where the transformative power of love can genuinely thrive.

Demonstrating the transformative
power of forgiveness

In the book of Mark, a pivotal narrative is found in the passages that describe the baptism of Jesus. This event unveils a profound truth about the nature of love and its correlation with the spirits that surround us. Just as Jesus emerged from the waters of baptism, divested of any detrimental influences, we too can experience the purity of love when we rid ourselves of negative energies and harmful influences.

By aligning our lives with the spirit of love, as exemplified by Jesus' transformative experience, we create an environment where love can flourish effortlessly. The act of letting go of certain spirits, as referred to in the context of Mark, refers to distancing ourselves from attitudes, behaviors, and relationships that impede the free flow of genuine love.

My ministry underscores that the essence of love becomes clear and attainable when we consciously choose to surround ourselves with positive influences, shedding those spirits that hinder its expression. By doing so, we lay the groundwork for profound connections, authentic relationships, and a nurturing atmosphere where the transformative power of love can genuinely thrive.

There was a profound instance in my journey where the teachings I espouse illuminated the transformative potency of forgiveness. I encountered situations where individuals treated me in ways that seemed contrary to the essence of being a child of God. Despite these hurtful experiences, I found myself drawn to a fundamental principle rooted in the scriptures.

In the book of Mark, there lies a passage that resonates deeply with this situation. Jesus imparts the wisdom that 'if you do not forgive, neither will your Father in heaven forgive your trespasses.' This message underscored the profound interconnectedness between extending forgiveness and receiving divine forgiveness.

Considering this teaching, I embarked on a journey of prayer and introspection. Recognizing that we are all fallible beings in need of grace, I chose to pray for those who had treated me with less kindness. I understood that forgiving them was not just a matter of personal growth, but a reflection of my own willingness to align with the principles of divine love and forgiveness.

The transformative power of forgiveness became evident as I experienced a profound shift within myself. By extending forgiveness, I not only released the burden of resentment but also created space for healing and growth. This act of embracing forgiveness, as guided by the teachings of Mark, enabled me to transcend the hurtful experiences and foster a renewed sense of compassion and empathy.

This instance serves as a testament to the timeless wisdom encapsulated in the scriptures. It demonstrates that the act of forgiving others, even when they have treated us poorly, not only bridges human divides but also resonates with the divine call for reconciliation and restoration. The teachings of Mark provide a guiding light in navigating the intricate terrain of forgiveness, empowering us to transform pain into a journey towards spiritual upliftment and profound connection.

Encouraging members to cultivate empathy in their interactions with others.

When it comes to nurturing empathy within the interactions of my members, I often turn to the wisdom encapsulated in Ephesians 6:10-15, a passage I refer to as "spirit-filled warfare." Let me elaborate further to provide clarity:

In Ephesians 6:10-15, the apostle Paul imparts a profound lesson that resonates deeply with the cultivation of empathy. He speaks of spiritual armor, a metaphorical representation of the virtues and qualities we need to navigate life's challenges. This spiritual armor, which includes the breastplate of righteousness and the readiness of the gospel of peace, carries immense relevance to the concept of empathy.

Empathy, you see, is a form of spiritual armor. It acts as a breastplate, guarding our hearts against the divisive forces of misunderstanding and indifference. Just as a breastplate provides protection to the core of our being, empathy safeguards the core of our humanity, fostering connections and understanding even in the face of differences.

The readiness of the gospel of peace, as mentioned in Ephesians, aligns beautifully with the practice of empathy. Just as we prepare ourselves for spiritual warfare by being ready to embrace peace, we prepare ourselves for genuine connections by cultivating an attitude of empathetic understanding. Empathy allows us to approach others with a heart of peace, seeking to understand their perspectives and emotions, and promoting harmony rather than discord.

Furthermore, the term "spirit-filled warfare" underscores the significance of empathy in our daily battles against discord and disconnection. Empathy serves as a potent weapon against misunderstanding and division, allowing us to bridge gaps, heal wounds, and bring about transformative change.

Therefore, in encouraging my followers to cultivate empathy, I guide them to embrace the principles of spirit-filled warfare outlined in Ephesians. I emphasize that the battles we face are not merely external, but also internal and relational. Empathy becomes our armor, our shield, and our weapon, enabling us to engage with others in ways that bring about unity, understanding, and the love that transcends all barriers. Just as the armor of Ephesians fortifies the spiritual warrior, empathy fortifies the bonds between individuals and fosters a more compassionate and interconnected world.

Anecdotes that illustrate bonds.

Let me share an anecdote that shows the profound bonds I've been speaking of – connections that stand the test of time and are nurtured by love, forgiveness, and empathy.

There have been many parishioners whom I had the privilege of counseling many years ago. Many have experienced brokenness and were burdened by a deep-seated resentment toward estranged relationships. The wounds of agony and pain were still raw, and the relationship between them was fractured beyond repair, or so many thoughts.

Through our sessions, I encouraged various members to embrace the teachings of love, forgiveness, and empathy that are fundamental to my ministry. Drawing inspiration from the scriptural principles we've discussed; they embarked on a journey to release the heavy baggage of resentment and pain they carried.

Over time, the relationship between many that I helped transformed. They began to rebuild their connection with a foundation of love and understanding, letting go of past grievances. The bond that blossomed between them was truly transformative – a testament to the enduring strength of empathy, forgiveness, and love.

Approaching relationships and friendships based on conventional teachings.

Trust is important to me. When contemplating my approach to relationships and friendships, I find profound guidance in the timeless wisdom of Proverbs 27:6, which states, 'Wounds from a friend can be trusted, but an enemy multiplies kisses.' This verse resonates deeply with the principles that underpin the bonds of trust and authenticity within genuine friendships.

This proverb delves into the essence of true companionship by highlighting the indispensable role of trust. Within the context of relationships, it acknowledges that genuine friends are not mere yes-men or flatterers. Rather, they possess the courage and integrity to address even the most delicate matters with sincerity and candor. Their intentions are born out of love and concern, and their words, though they may be difficult to hear, carry the weight of genuine care for our well-being.

A deeper understanding of this proverb reveals that the 'wounds' inflicted by a friend are not intended to cause harm, but rather to facilitate growth, learning, and improvement. A sincere friend recognizes the value of offering constructive criticism or guidance, even when it may temporarily sting. Such feedback is rooted in a desire to see us evolve, to overcome challenges, and to become the best versions of ourselves.

Conversely, the mention of an 'enemy multiplying kisses' alludes to the dangers of insincere or superficial relationships. It warns against those who shower us with flattery and empty gestures while concealing malicious intent. This contrast underscores the importance of discernment in choosing the company we keep, as well as the authenticity and depth that define true friendships.

My approach to relationships and friendships is deeply rooted in the principles set forth by this proverb. I encourage the cultivation of bonds that rest on trust, transparency, and a shared commitment to growth. Genuine friends are those who are willing to traverse the uncomfortable territories of vulnerability and honesty, confident that the foundation of love and concern will remain unshaken.

By embracing the spirit of Proverbs 27:6, we nurture relationships that stand as a testament to the transformative power of authentic connections – bonds that not only endure the tests of time but also enrich our lives immeasurably.

Want to maintain a healthy and meaningful relationship?

"When it comes to nurturing healthy and meaningful relationships, particularly in the face of adversity, I often turn to the metaphor of 'putting on the full armor of God.' Allow me to delve deeper into what this means and how it can guide us through challenging times.

The concept of the full armor of God is drawn from the biblical passage in Ephesians 6:10-18, where the apostle Paul uses the imagery of a warrior's armor to convey the spiritual virtues and principles that empower us to navigate life's trials. Let's break down each element of this armor and relate it to maintaining relationships:

The Belt of Truth: Just as a belt holds a warrior's armor together, truth serves as the foundation of any healthy relationship. Honesty, transparency, and genuine communication are essential to fostering trust and intimacy, even when facing difficult circumstances.

The Breastplate of Righteousness: Just as a breastplate protects the heart, righteousness safeguards our intentions and actions. In relationships, maintaining integrity and doing what is right ensures that our interactions are rooted in respect and honor.

The Shoes of Peace: As shoes provide stability and mobility, the pursuit of peace is crucial in relationships.

During challenging times, cultivating a peaceful demeanor, and seeking resolution can prevent conflicts from escalating.

The Shield of Faith: A shield deflects attacks, and faith acts as our shield against negativity and doubt. Trusting in the strength of our relationships and remaining steadfast in our commitment can help us weather storms together.

The Helmet of Salvation: Just as a helmet protects the head, salvation serves as a reminder of our identity and worth. Recognizing our inherent value and that of others prevents us from succumbing to insecurities that might strain relationships.

The Sword of the Spirit: A sword symbolizes offensive and defensive power. The Word of God – which encompasses teachings of love, forgiveness, and empathy – equips us with the ability to combat misunderstandings and negativity while nurturing understanding and connection.

Prayer and Supplication: Prayer connects us to a higher source of wisdom and strength. Seeking divine guidance in our relationships allows us to approach challenges with a humble and open heart.

In the context of relationships, 'putting on the full armor of God' means embodying these virtues and principles. It's about approaching interactions with truth, integrity, peace, trust, self-worth, and a commitment to growth. This armor enables us to overcome obstacles, extend empathy, offer forgiveness, and maintain a foundation of love even in trying times.

So, my advice for maintaining healthy and meaningful relationships during challenging times is to internalize and embody the virtues encapsulated in the armor of God. By doing so, we equip ourselves to navigate difficulties with grace, humility, and an unwavering commitment to the well-being of those we cherish.

Human connection + Love = a theological or
philosophical foundation?

Absolutely, the teachings on human connection and love that I hold dear are deeply rooted in both theological and philosophical foundations. These core principles have been instilled in me through the invaluable guidance of my mother and the formative experiences I gained from the church I grew up in, situated in the quaint town of McCormick, South Carolina.

From a theological standpoint, my mother imparted profound insights into the essence of love as a divine gift and a universal virtue. Her teachings resonated with the overarching message of compassion, forgiveness, and empathy that underpin many religious traditions. These teachings reinforced the idea that love transcends boundaries, serving as a powerful force that unites humanity in its shared journey.

In the nurturing environment of the Betany Church, I was raised in, I absorbed essential philosophical foundations concerning the interconnectedness of all beings. The theological messages of grace, redemption, and the transformative power of love were interwoven with philosophical concepts emphasizing the inherent dignity and worth of every individual. These teachings solidified my understanding that genuine human connection is an embodiment of the divine's love for us, and our responsibility to extend that love to others.

Together, the amalgamation of my mother's teachings and the spiritual upbringing I received in my hometown church formed the bedrock of my approach to fostering human connection and love. These influences underscored the significance of empathy, understanding, and the profound bonds that are cultivated through acts of kindness, forgiveness, and sincere concern for one another. They remind me that in embracing love and nurturing meaningful connections, we participate in a timeless and universal journey that enriches the very fabric of human existence.

Ministry and the community respond to teachings on love, forgiveness, and empathy.

The response to my teachings on love, forgiveness, and empathy within both my ministry and the community has been truly heartwarming. Individuals have consistently shown us an outpouring of love and appreciation. It's incredibly humbling to witness how these teachings resonate with people on a personal level and become guiding principles in their lives.

In our ministry, we've witnessed profound transformations as individuals embrace the tenets of love, forgiveness, and empathy. Members of the community have shared stories of healing relationships that were once strained, of finding solace and peace through the power of forgiveness, and of experiencing the warmth of genuine empathy in times of need. These teachings have not only deepened their connection to their faith but have also enriched their relationships with one another and the wider world.

Furthermore, our vision for the church to become a full-service institution and a true friend to the community has garnered significant support and enthusiasm. As we've embarked on this journey, we've seen our church become a hub of positive change, offering resources, support, and a safe space for everyone. This expansion of our role in the community has allowed us to channel the principles of love, forgiveness, and empathy into tangible actions that address real needs.

Through initiatives like community service projects, support programs, and outreach efforts, we've witnessed firsthand how the teachings we hold dear can manifest in the betterment of lives. The impact is evident in the smiling faces of those who have received assistance, the renewed hope of individuals who felt forgotten, and the unity that emerges when a community comes together with shared values.

The teachings on love, forgiveness, and empathy have not only resonated with individuals in our ministry and community but have also fostered a collective spirit of compassion and empowerment. It's a beautiful testament to the transformative power of these principles, not only in individuals' personal lives but also in the larger tapestry of our shared human experience.

Supporting Sciptures for Section III

Here are some scriptures that we can rely on that will support this section:

The Bible provides valuable insights into the complexities of relationships and friendships, emphasizing the importance of love, trust, and mutual respect. Here are some scriptures that highlight the significance of these threads in our interactions with others:

1 Corinthians 13:4-7 (NIV) "Love is patient, love is kind. It does not envy, it does not boast, it is not proud. It does not dishonor others, it is not self-seeking, it is

not easily angered, it keeps no record of wrongs. Love does not delight in evil but rejoices with the truth. It always protects, always trusts, always hopes, always perseveres."

This famous passage from the "love chapter" of the Bible beautifully encapsulates the essence of love in relationships and friendships. It underscores the qualities of love, such as patience, kindness, trust, and forgiveness, which form the foundation of strong, enduring connections.

Proverbs 17:17 (NIV) "A friend loves at all times, and a brother is born for a time of adversity."

This verse speaks to the loyalty and constancy of true friendships. Friends who love at all times and offer support during difficult moments are precious gifts in the complexities of life.

Proverbs 18:24 (NIV) "One who has unreliable friends soon comes to ruin, but there is a friend who sticks closer than a brother."

This verse cautions against unreliable friendships while emphasizing the significance of those who remain steadfast and faithful in challenging times.

John 15:13 (NIV) "Greater love has no one than this: to lay down one's life for one's friends."

Jesus' words remind us of the sacrificial nature of love and the willingness to put the needs of friends before our own. Selflessness and genuine care are integral to strong relationships and friendships.

Ecclesiastes 4:9-10 (NIV) "Two are better than one because they have a good return for their labor: If either of them falls down, one can help the other up. But pity anyone who falls and has no one to help them up."

This passage highlights the value of companionship and support in navigating the complexities of life. True friends are there to lift us up when we stumble, providing a sense of comfort and encouragement.

Proverbs 27:6 (NIV) "Wounds from a friend can be trusted, but an enemy multiplies kisses.

This verse emphasizes the importance of trust in genuine friendships. True friends are willing to address difficult issues honestly, even if it involves constructive criticism or guidance, and their intentions are rooted in love and concern.

These scriptures reveal the significance of love, trust, and selflessness in the intricacies of relationships and friendships. By applying these timeless principles, we can strengthen our connections with others and foster lasting bonds built on mutual respect and care.

Section IV: Complexity in the Ministry – Nurturing Souls, Embracing Humanity

As a pastor of a non-denominational church, Dr. Tompkins bore the sacred responsibility of guiding souls and embracing the diverse tapestry of humanity. This segment will illuminate the challenges and joys of the ministry, exploring how his devotion to God translated into dedicated service to his congregation. From officiating sacred ceremonies to providing spiritual support during times of crisis, his experiences will reveal the profound impact of faith and compassion on the lives of those he touched.

For Dr. Tompkins, the ministry was both a sacred duty and a profound privilege. As we explore the world of spiritual guidance and communal support, we witness how his faith provided strength and guidance amidst the complexities of ministerial responsibilities.

David provides information how his work in the ministry connects to his faith and how he sees it as both a sacred duty and profound privilege for him as a servant of God:

Defining the concept of a sacred duty

In the context of Paul's teachings in the New Testament of the Bible, compassion is a key concept that aligns with his emphasis on love, empathy, and caring for one another. Paul often spoke about the importance of showing compassion and kindness towards others, both within the Christian community and beyond.

One of the most well-known passages where Paul discusses compassion is in his letter to the Colossians, specifically Colossians 3:12-14 (NIV):

Therefore, as God's chosen people, holy and dearly loved, clothe yourselves with compassion, kindness, humility, gentleness and patience. Bear with each other and forgive one another if any of you has a grievance against someone. Forgive as the Lord forgave you. And over all these virtues put on love, which binds them all together in perfect unity.

Here, Paul encourages believers to embody qualities such as compassion, kindness, and forgiveness in their interactions with others. He emphasizes that these virtues are not only reflective of God's character but also contribute to the unity and well-being of the Christian community.

When dealing with parishioners who are experiencing brokenness, Paul's teachings on compassion can provide a guiding framework for pastors and leaders:

Empathy and Understanding: Compassion involves understanding the suffering and challenges faced by others. Paul's teachings encourage believers to put themselves in the shoes of those who are struggling, showing empathy and a willingness to listen and support.

Practical Assistance: Compassion goes beyond mere sentiment; it involves taking practical steps to help those in need. Paul's emphasis on kindness and humility encourages believers to provide tangible assistance to those who are hurting, whether it's through emotional support, prayer, or practical help.

Forgiveness and Restoration: In cases of brokenness, Paul's teachings on forgiveness are relevant. Just as God forgave through Christ, believers are encouraged to offer forgiveness and facilitate the process of healing and restoration for those who are broken.

Building a Supportive Community: Paul's vision of the church as a united body underscores the importance of creating a supportive and caring community. Compassion plays a crucial role in fostering an environment where individuals feel safe to share their struggles and find acceptance and encouragement.

Modeling Christ's Love: Ultimately, Paul's teachings on compassion are rooted in Christ's example. Jesus showed immense compassion towards those who were marginalized, sick, and broken. Following this example, believers are called to embody Christ's love and compassion in their interactions with others.

In summary, compassion is a central theme in Paul's teachings, and it plays a vital role in guiding how Christians should relate to one another and respond to the brokenness experienced by parishioners. By embodying compassion, leaders and members of the church can create an environment of healing, support, and spiritual growth for those who are going through difficult times. This is something I will never stop teaching.

Moments that have reaffirmed the ministry as a privilege.

There are examples of moments that could reaffirm the idea of ministry as a "profound privilege," especially when dealing with parishioners who have experienced addiction, divorce, and obsessions.

Recovery and Transformation from Addiction: There has been a parishioner who struggled with a severe addiction for years. Through the ministry's support, counseling, and prayers, this individual managed to overcome their addiction and rebuild their life. As the person's pastor I have able to witness this transformation, from the depths of despair to a life of sobriety and purpose, reaffirmed the privilege of being part of a community that aids in healing and renewal. To witness their recovery, to see them emerge from the grips of addiction and find a renewed sense of purpose, has affirmed for me that our ministry is a true privilege. We get to be instruments of God's grace, guiding people through their darkest moments towards a brighter future.

Guiding Through Divorce and Healing: The ministry provided a safe space for a couple within the congregation that faced a painful divorce for them to heal, offering counseling and support as they navigated the emotional and spiritual challenges of the process. Eventually, both individuals found healing and were able to co-parent with a newfound sense of understanding. This example could emphasize the ministry's role in guiding people through broken relationships and helping them find hope amidst heartache.

In the midst of a couple's painful divorce, our ministry was able to provide a haven of understanding and healing. To witness this couple, who once faced bitterness and pain, now communicating with empathy, and working together for the well-being of their children, reaffirms the deep privilege we have in our ministry. We have the opportunity to bring light to some of life's darkest moments.

Overcoming Obsessions and Finding Spiritual Renewal: There has been an individual who struggled with consuming obsessions that were impacting their spiritual life. Through the ministry's guidance and prayer support, this person was able to gain control over their obsessions and rediscover a deeper connection with their faith. This example could highlight the role of the ministry in providing a path to spiritual renewal and personal growth.

Through our ministry's commitment to understanding, compassion, and prayer, this individual found the strength to break free from those chains and experience a renewed sense of faith and purpose. Such experiences remind us that guiding others through their struggles is a profound privilege that fills our hearts with purpose.

By sharing real-life stories of transformation and healing, I hope I was able to illustrate the idea of ministry as a profound privilege. These examples demonstrate how the ministry can make a lasting impact on individuals' lives during their moments of greatest need, reinforcing the idea that serving others in their brokenness is a sacred calling.

Examples of moments or experiences that have reaffirmed the idea of my ministry as a profound privilege.

When I say, "Deliverance is a lifestyle; not a circumstance," I am expressing a profound insight about the nature of spiritual freedom and growth. This statement suggests that the concept of deliverance goes beyond being a one-time event or a response to specific circumstances; rather, it's a continuous journey and way of living that involves ongoing transformation, healing, and alignment with God's will. Let's break down the meaning of this statement and how it relates to scriptures.

Deliverance as a Lifestyle: I am emphasizing that deliverance, which often refers to being set free from spiritual bondage, addictions, negative thought patterns, or other obstacles, is not something that happens just once and is then complete. Instead, it's an ongoing process that requires consistent effort, renewal, and dedication to living in alignment with

God's truth. It's about cultivating a daily walk with God, making choices that reflect my principles, and continually seeking my guidance and transformation in all aspects of life.

Not a Circumstance: By saying "not a circumstance," I am suggesting that deliverance isn't just a reaction to external situations or emergencies. It's not just a response to crisis. Instead, it's a fundamental way of approaching life, rooted in a deep relationship with God. This perspective encourages individuals to proactively engage with their spiritual growth, consistently seeking God's presence, and aligning their thoughts, behaviors, and decisions with His will.

Relating to Scriptures: This concept of deliverance as a lifestyle resonates with various teachings in the Bible. For example:

Romans 12:2 (NIV): "Do not conform to the pattern of this world but be transformed by the renewing of your mind. Then you will be able to test and approve what God's will is—his good, pleasing and perfect will." This verse highlights the ongoing process of transformation that happens through renewing the mind, which aligns with the idea of deliverance as a continuous journey.

Galatians 5:1 (NIV): "It is for freedom that Christ has set us free. Stand firm, then, and do not let yourselves be burdened again by a yoke of slavery." This verse speaks to the freedom we have in Christ, emphasizing the importance of actively living in that freedom rather than returning to old patterns.

Philippians 2:12-13 (NIV): "Therefore, my dear friends, as you have always obeyed—not only in my presence but now much more in my absence—continue to work out your salvation with fear and trembling, for it is God who works in you to will and to act in order to fulfill his good purpose." This passage encourages believers to continually work out their salvation, which relates to the idea of deliverance as an ongoing process.

In summary, my statement "Deliverance is a lifestyle; not a circumstance", underscores the idea that spiritual freedom and transformation are not isolated events but rather integral components of a Christian's daily life. It's about actively living out the principles of faith, renewal, and alignment with God's will on a continuous basis, drawing strength from the relationship with God and the guidance of His Word.

Being a pastor vs. a balancing act

When I say, "By not taking anything personal," he is expressing a principle of emotional detachment and objectivity in his role as a pastor. This concept is drawn from a perspective often associated with effective leadership and interpersonal relationships. Let's explore what he likely means by this and how it relates to balancing the spiritual and administrative aspects of his role:

Emotional Detachment: By not taking anything personally, I am suggesting that I try to avoid allowing personal emotions, sensitivities, or ego-driven reactions to cloud his judgment or influence my decisions. In a pastoral role, I am likely to interact with a wide range of individuals who have diverse needs, opinions, and circumstances. Embracing emotional detachment means that I strive to approach situations with a clear and impartial mindset, focusing on the best interests of the congregation and the organization.

Objective Decision-Making: When I say I don't take things personally, I am emphasizing the importance of making decisions based on a higher perspective rather than getting caught up in personal reactions. This approach enables him to consider the greater good, the values and mission of the church, and the well-being of the community he serves. It helps me to avoid making hasty or biased decisions that could be influenced by personal feelings.

Reducing Conflict: Taking nothing personally can also help reduce conflicts and misunderstandings. When faced with criticism, differing opinions, or challenging situations, this approach allows me to respond calmly and thoughtfully rather than reacting defensively or emotionally. This can contribute to healthier interactions and more effective conflict resolution.

Balancing Spiritual and Administrative Aspects: The role of a pastor involves both spiritual leadership and administrative responsibilities. By not taking things personally, again, I am indicating that I strive to approach administrative tasks, organizational challenges, and interpersonal interactions with a sense of equanimity. This enables me to focus on the spiritual aspects of his role without being overwhelmed by administrative stresses or interpersonal conflicts.

My' approach to not taking anything personally speaks to my commitment to maintaining a sense of emotional equilibrium and objectivity. It allows me to navigate the complexities of my pastoral role while keeping me focused on the spiritual well-being of the congregation and the larger mission of the church. This principle aligns with the idea of servant leadership, where leaders prioritize the needs of others and the greater good over personal reactions or ego-driven concerns.

Nurturing souls translates into practical actions.

My' approach of nurturing souls through practical actions such as providing training, seminars, and teaching parishioners how to face their situations without pride can have a transformative impact on his congregation. Let's explore how these actions strengthen the congregation:

Training and Seminars: By offering training sessions and seminars, I am equipping my congregation with practical skills, knowledge, and tools to navigate various challenges in their lives. These sessions could cover topics such as communication, conflict resolution, emotional well-being, financial stewardship, and spiritual growth. When individuals are empowered with practical insights and strategies, they gain a sense of self-efficacy and confidence in dealing with life's complexities.

Facing Situations Without Pride: Teaching parishioners to face their situations without pride is a valuable lesson in humility, vulnerability, and self-awareness. This approach encourages individuals to acknowledge their limitations, seek help when needed, and embrace a teachable spirit. By addressing pride, I can help create a culture of openness and authenticity within the congregation, where members can support each other without fear of judgment.

Strengthening Community Bonds: Through training, seminars, and humility-focused teaching, I can foster a sense of unity and community within the congregation. As individuals engage in shared learning experiences and open conversations about their challenges, they form deeper connections with one another. This sense of belonging and mutual support strengthens the congregation's bonds and encourages an atmosphere of trust.

Holistic Growth: The practical skills acquired through training and the mindset of humility contribute to the holistic growth of congregation members. They are not only spiritually nourished but also equipped to handle real-world situations with wisdom and grace. This balanced approach to personal development helps individuals flourish in all areas of their lives.

Effective Problem Solving: When parishioners are taught how to approach their challenges without pride, they are more likely to seek constructive solutions rather than becoming defensive or stuck in unproductive patterns. This promotes effective problem-solving and a willingness to work collaboratively towards resolutions.

Cultivating a Culture of Learning: My emphasis on training and humility fosters a culture of continuous learning and growth within the congregation. Members are encouraged to be curious, open-minded, and receptive to new insights. This culture of learning can lead to personal development, spiritual maturity, and a willingness to adapt to changing circumstances.

Modeling Leadership by Example: By embodying the principles he teaches; Dr. Tompkins sets an example for his congregation. His own humility, willingness to learn, and commitment to practical growth inspire others to follow suit. This form of leadership by example can have a ripple effect throughout the congregation.

In summary, my approach of providing practical training, seminars, and teaching humility-based principles creates an environment that empowers individuals to thrive emotionally, spiritually, and practically. It strengthens the congregation by fostering unity, enhancing problem-solving skills, nurturing holistic growth, and cultivating a culture of learning and humility.

Embracing the diverse tapestry of humanity

Embracing the diverse tapestry of humanity within my congregation and community has been a cornerstone of my ministry. While I encountered the significance of diversity early on in my journey, I have consistently sought meaningful connections with parishioners and individuals from all walks of life.

I have actively cultivated an environment where every voice is heard and valued. This involves intentionally reaching out to individuals who might have different backgrounds, experiences, and perspectives. Through personal conversations, community events, and targeted outreach, I aim to bridge gaps and build bridges of understanding.

Understanding that God's love transcends all boundaries, I strive to create a safe space where individuals from various cultural, ethnic, and socioeconomic backgrounds feel welcomed and embraced. I encourage open dialogues that celebrate our differences and promote empathy. Diversity is not just a buzzword; it's a beautiful reality that enriches our spiritual journey.

In addition to connecting on a personal level, I have integrated diverse perspectives into our teachings and worship. This allows us to gain deeper insights into the richness of God's creation and our shared humanity. I am committed to ensuring that our congregation reflects the broader community we serve, and this commitment is reflected in our programming, events, and outreach efforts.

I find inspiration in the fact that God is a 'people person.' His unconditional love extends to everyone, regardless of their background. In emulating His example, I continue to strive for a congregation and community where unity is strengthened through our diversity, and where we grow together in our understanding of what it means to be children of God.

Ways the ministry has been
tested during times of crisis

One of the most profound tests our ministry encountered was during the onset of the COVID-19 pandemic. Like many others, we were faced with unprecedented challenges that required us to adapt, innovate, and find new ways to serve our congregation and community.

In response to the pandemic, we made the difficult decision to temporarily close our physical doors to ensure the safety and well-being of our members. This was a trying time as we navigated uncharted waters, grappling with the uncertainties and anxieties that the pandemic brought. However, within this adversity, we saw an opportunity to strengthen our bonds as a community and reaffirm our commitment to our mission.

Closing our doors physically did not mean closing our hearts or our connection to our congregation. We quickly pivoted to virtual platforms, offering online worship services, prayer gatherings, and study groups. This transition wasn't without its challenges, but it was a testament to the resilience and adaptability of our congregation.

The most remarkable outcome of this trial was the unexpected blessing of building a brand-new church amid the tribulation. In the face of the pandemic, we embarked on a journey to create a space that would not only accommodate our congregation's needs but also reflect the unity and hope that defined our response to the crisis.

Through the collective efforts and unwavering faith of our members, we turned what could have been a setback into a remarkable opportunity for growth. With determination, we raised the funds, secured the resources, and worked together to construct a new church that stands as a symbol of our community's strength and resilience.

This experience affirmed our belief that challenges, no matter how daunting, can be transformed into catalysts for positive change. We learned the importance of staying connected, adapting to new circumstances, and focusing on the greater purpose that unites us. Our journey through the pandemic strengthened our sense of unity and deepened our commitment to serving one another and our community.

Looking back, I am humbled by the journey we undertook. Our response to the COVID-19 crisis reminded us that the church is not confined to a physical building but resides within the hearts of its members. Together, we weathered the storm, grew in our faith, and emerged stronger than before—a testament to the power of God's grace and the resilience of the human spirit.

Congregations and readers understand.

What I deeply wish for my congregation and readers to grasp is the profound impact that faith and compassion can have on the lives of those we've had the privilege to touch. At the core of everything we do is the principle of love—love that extends beyond boundaries, categories, and differences. It's a love that reaches across the board, connecting us to one another in the most meaningful and authentic way.

Faith, the cornerstone of our spiritual journey, guides us to a place of unwavering trust and hope. It's this faith that propels us to extend our hearts and hands to those who need it most. In doing so, we come to realize that our actions carry the potential to transform lives, to offer solace in times of despair, and to inspire a sense of belonging even during adversity.

Compassion is the heartbeat of our ministry. It's the bridge that connects us on a human level, reminding us that every individual we encounter is a soul deserving of kindness, understanding, and support. This compassion isn't selective—it's all-encompassing, recognizing the shared humanity that unites us all. It means standing with the broken, lifting the fallen, and embracing the overlooked.

In a world that often emphasizes differences and divisions, I want to stress the significance of finding common ground—a place where we can love everyone the same. This common ground is not rooted in the superficial, but rather in our shared values, dreams, and the universal desire for connection and meaning. It's about acknowledging that, beneath the surface, we are all seeking purpose and belonging.

When we walk the path of love, faith, and compassion, we see lives transformed. We witness individuals finding hope amidst despair, strength in the face of adversity, and healing from wounds that run deep. We create a community that becomes a haven for the weary and a source of inspiration for the lost.

What I hope to convey is that our actions matter. The love we show, the faith we hold, and the compassion we extend—they are all building blocks of a legacy that can shape destinies and touch souls. Together, we can make a difference in the lives of others and, in doing so, experience a depth of fulfillment and purpose that only a life rooted in faith, love, and compassion can bring."

Supporting Sciptures for Section 1V

Here are a variety of resources that supports this section:

The Bible contains numerous scriptures that provide guidance and inspiration for those engaged in the ministry of nurturing souls and embracing humanity. Here are some verses that emphasize the significance of compassion, service, and love in this sacred calling:

Matthew 20:28 (NIV) "Just as the Son of Man did not come to be served, but to serve, and to give his life as a ransom for many."

This verse exemplifies the heart of the ministry, which is centered on service and self-sacrifice. Embracing humanity requires a willingness to serve others with humility and love, following the example set by Jesus.

Mark 10:45 (NIV) "For even the Son of Man did not come to be served, but to serve, and to give his life as a ransom for many."

Similar to the previous verse, Mark 10:45 reiterates Jesus' purpose of selfless service. Ministers are called to follow His example and serve with compassion, leading others towards spiritual growth and transformation.

Galatians 5:13 (NIV) "You, my brothers and sisters, were called to be free. But do not use your freedom to indulge the flesh; rather, serve one another humbly in love."

This verse emphasizes the importance of serving others with love and humility. In the ministry, the focus is on nurturing souls and helping people experience the freedom that comes from a relationship with God.

1 Peter 4:10 (NIV) "Each of you should use whatever gift you have received to serve others, as faithful stewards of God's grace in its various forms."

Ministers are encouraged to use their unique gifts and talents to serve others and extend God's grace. Embracing humanity involves recognizing the diversity of God's creation and offering support and compassion to all.

Romans 12:10 (NIV) "Be devoted to one another in love. Honor one another above yourselves."
Ministry involves building genuine and loving relationships with others. This verse reminds us to treat others with honor and love, nurturing souls through authentic connections and compassionate care.

2 Corinthians 1:3-4 (NIV) "Praise be to the God and Father of our Lord Jesus Christ, the Father of compassion and the God of all comfort, who comforts us in all our troubles so that we can comfort those in any trouble with the comfort we ourselves receive from God."
Ministers are called to be channels of God's comfort and compassion to those in need. By extending understanding and support, they help individuals find solace and healing in challenging times.

These scriptures highlight the essence of the ministry - to nurture souls and embrace humanity with compassion, service, and love. By drawing on these timeless principles, ministers can fulfill.

their sacred calling, guiding others towards spiritual growth and a deeper connection with God.

Section V: Complexity in Brokenness and Resilience-
The Unyielding Spirit

Life's journey is seldom without moments of profound brokenness. In this closing section, we will bear witness to Bishop Tompkins' own trials and tribulations, and how he navigated the darkest corners of despair. In the face of adversity, he found resilience and the transformative power of faith to heal wounded hearts.

Dr. Tompkins provides information that he learned from others about being broken by life's trials and tribulations and how all of this connects to his faith and how he sees life. He also talks about why there is a concern and how this effects all Christians that say they are a servant of God:

In the pages that follow, Dr.Tompkins will lead us through life's grand tapestry, weaving together the threads of business, religion, relationships, friendships, ministry, and the unyielding spirit in brokenness. His experiences and reflections shall serve as guiding lights, illuminating our own paths as we seek purpose, understanding, and solace in a world that often defies comprehension.

Let us embark on this transformative odyssey together, walking side by side with a man of God, whose life exemplifies the profound enigma of the Complexity Form that shapes us all. As seekers of truth, stewards of love, and believers in the resiliency of the human spirit, we shall uncover the beauty that lies within life's intricate design.

Key moments of brokenness

"Until I learned how to let moments in life play out, that is when I understood that brokenness brings blessing," I suggest that we learned to accept and embrace the challenging moments or "broken" aspects of life instead of trying to resist or control them. By doing so, I discovered that these difficult moments could lead to positive outcomes or "blessings".

I am emphasizing the idea that personal growth and resilience can be born out of adversity and difficult experiences. Instead of avoiding or fearing brokenness, I learned to see it as an integral part of the human experience and an opportunity for learning and growth.

Life's most profound lessons often come from moments of brokenness, teaching us resilience, empathy, and the strength to rebuild God's unchanging hands.

By allowing life's challenges to unfold naturally, I discovered that even in my most broken moments, there was a hidden beauty waiting to be uncovered that Jesus has been here all along to lift up. In the end, I've come to appreciate that the journey from brokenness to blessing is a testament to the human spirit's capacity for transformation because gain something much better and stronger…which leads to a connection with God. These alternative closings emphasize the transformative power of embracing life's challenges and finding blessings in moments of brokenness.

Faith playing a role in trials and tribulations.

I've always had my faith in gear even in the most challenging trials and tribulations. It's been a guiding light throughout my life, providing me with strength and resilience. I've encountered numerous self-teaching and teachable moments where I had to take a dose of my own medicine, reminding myself that God would never put more on me than I could bear. There were times when I felt overwhelmed, but my faith served as a steadfast anchor, helping me find purpose and meaning during adversity. It's in those moments of deepest despair that I've witnessed the true power of faith, as it not only sustained me but also allowed me to emerge from the darkness with newfound wisdom and a stronger connection to my spirituality. Through faith, I've learned that even in the most broken times, there is a path to healing and growth, and it's a testament to the unwavering love and support of a higher power.

The insights I've gained from others who have walked the path of brokenness have been invaluable to my own journey. I've had the privilege of listening to countless stories of resilience, strength, and unwavering faith in the face of adversity. These experiences have not only enriched my understanding but have also served as a wellspring of inspiration. When I teach and share these stories, I emphasize the importance of confronting the truth, no matter how painful it may be, because it's in facing our truths that we find the strength to heal and grow.

These stories have not only ministered to those I teach but have also ministered unto me. They have reminded me that we are all on unique journeys, and there is purpose in every step we take, even in the most challenging times. Through the stories of others, I've seen how God's grace and love shine through even the darkest moments. They have reinforced my belief that there is a divine plan for each of us, and it's our resilience and faith that carry us through the storms. So, I continue to draw strength from the shared experiences of others, and it reaffirms my conviction that we are never alone in our struggles and that there is always hope, even in the most trying time.

Concerned about brokenness

There is a significant concern about the impact of brokenness on Christians who identify as servants of God. The reason for this concern lies in the very essence of being a servant. To truly serve, one must be willing to decrease themselves. Being a servant involves giving more of yourself, your time, your compassion, and your love to others and to God's work. However, it's important to understand that you cannot be a genuine servant until you've wrestled with and overcome the issues causing your own brokenness.

The struggle to give up what is causing the brokenness is not an easy one. It often involves confronting deep-seated fears, doubts, and vulnerabilities. It means acknowledging one's own wounds and limitations. But here's where the profound lesson lies in that struggle, we learn the true essence of humility and empathy. We learn to extend grace to ourselves as we extend it to others. We discover that our brokenness can be transformed into a source of strength and compassion.

In serving despite our brokenness, we come to understand that our imperfections do not disqualify us from being instruments of God's grace; they make us relatable and authentic in our ministry. We learn that God's power is made perfect in our weakness. So, the concern about the impact of brokenness on servants of God teaches us that true service requires self-awareness, humility, and a willingness to turn our brokenness into a vessel of healing and hope for others.

Integrating the sha-bang

Integrating the various aspects of life into a journey towards resilience and healing is a multifaceted endeavor. It starts with a fundamental principle: passion must be interwoven into every aspect of your life. This means that your business should not merely be a profit-driven endeavor; it should be treated like a ministry where you serve not only your customers but your employees and community. Your relationships and friendships should be infused with the same sense of purpose, with the recognition that they are opportunities for growth, support, and mutual enrichment.

To achieve this integration, it's essential to approach each aspect of life with sincerity, recognizing that perfection is unattainable, but sincere effort is not. In your business, prioritize ethical practices and values that align with your faith and principles. In your relationships, foster a sense of connection and support that mirrors the love and compassion you find in ministry. In friendships, be genuine and empathetic, understanding that we all face challenges and imperfections.

Moreover, it's crucial to create a harmonious balance among these various aspects, ensuring that they complement each other rather than compete. Seek moments of alignment where your business goals, religious beliefs, and relationships converge, reinforcing your sense of purpose and direction. Ultimately, by treating all aspects of life as opportunities for sincere and passionate engagement, you can find resilience and healing in the midst of life's complexities.

My advice to readers facing their own moments of brokenness.

For those who find themselves in the midst of their own moments of brokenness and are seeking solace and understanding, I would offer this advice: You must develop a unique plan of self-criticism that is infused with kindness and patience. It's essential to start by acknowledging where you are in your journey without judgment or self-condemnation. Facing your trials of brokenness requires you to confront the issues at hand, but it also requires a gentle and compassionate approach towards yourself.

Begin by taking small steps toward self-discovery and healing. This might involve seeking support from trusted friends, family members, or a counselor who can provide a safe space for you to express your feelings and thoughts. It's crucial to remember that healing is not a linear process; it's okay to have setbacks and challenges along the way.

Additionally, consider incorporating practices that nurture your physical, mental, and spiritual well-being. This could include mindfulness meditation, journaling, prayer, or engaging in activities that bring you joy and peace. These practices can help you gain clarity and resilience as you navigate your journey through brokenness.

Be patient with yourself. Healing takes time, and there's no set timeline for overcoming brokenness. Embrace your vulnerabilities, for they are a part of what makes you uniquely human. Trust that, with kindness and self-compassion, you can emerge from your moments of brokenness stronger, wiser, and more resilient than before.

Experience and reflections
serve as guiding lights

My own experiences and reflections have been guiding lights throughout my journey. I've found that sincerity is the beacon that shines the brightest. Sincerity means being authentic and true to yourself, acknowledging your flaws, and embracing your strengths. It's with sincerity that I've navigated the complexities of brokenness and resilience.

By genuinely confronting my own struggles, I've been able to find the ministry I needed to move forward, and the help required to overcome adversity. This sincerity has led me to a deeper understanding of my purpose and a profound connection with my faith. It has illuminated my path, showing me that even in my most broken moments, there is a higher purpose at play.

To illuminate the paths of others seeking purpose and meaning, I would encourage them to start with self-reflection and honesty. Take the time to explore your own experiences, both the triumphs and the trials. Seek guidance from mentors, counselors, or spiritual leaders who can provide wisdom and support.

Embrace the idea that your journey is uniquely yours, and it's okay to ask for help along the way. Let sincerity be your guiding light, and as you move forward, you'll find that your experiences and reflections can not only bring you clarity and purpose but also serve as a source of inspiration and guidance for others on their own quests for meaning.

Lessons we can all draw

The complexities of life often present us with challenges, hurdles, and unexpected twists. However, within each of us, there resides an unyielding spirit, a beacon light that illuminates our path and provides the strength to face these complexities head-on.

One crucial lesson we can draw from this unyielding spirit is resilience. Life is not a smooth, straightforward journey; it's a tapestry of experiences that test our endurance and adaptability. The unyielding spirit within us reminds us that we have the capacity to overcome adversity, learn from setbacks, and emerge stronger. It teaches us that every complexity we encounter is an opportunity for growth.

Another lesson is the importance of faith and hope. In the face of life's complexities, our inner spirit encourages us to have faith in ourselves and in the journey ahead. It reminds us that even when circumstances seem insurmountable, there is always a glimmer of hope that can guide us through the darkest moments.

Additionally, our unyielding spirit teaches us the value of compassion and connection. It prompts us to reach out to others who may be facing their own complexities and offer support and understanding. In this way, we not only strengthen our own spirits but also contribute to the collective resilience of our communities.

The complexities of life and the unyielding spirit within us remind us that we are capable of far more than we may initially believe. They encourage us to embrace challenges as opportunities for growth, to hold onto faith and hope, and to extend compassion to ourselves and others. Through these lessons, we can navigate life's intricacies with grace and determination.

This transformative odyssey
& my concluding thoughts

As we conclude this transformative odyssey through the complexities of brokenness and resilience, I want to leave you with a profound sense of hope and purpose. Life, as we experience it, often reveals more than what meets the eye. It encompasses the depths of our emotions, the trials and tribulations that shape us, and the ever-evolving journey of self-discovery.

In times of hardship, remember that there is more to life than what you can see with your eyes alone. The challenges and obstacles you face are not insurmountable barriers but opportunities for growth and transformation. Embrace them as steppingstones on your path to resilience.

Moreover, there is more to life than simply seeking to be right with God, although faith and spirituality are powerful sources of strength. It's equally essential to find harmony within ourselves, to understand and heal our own wounds, and to nurture our emotional and mental well-being. By doing so, we can unlock our true potential and bring positive change to our lives.

Think about the story of Job from the Bible. Despite losing everything he held dear, he clung to his faith and remained resilient. His story teaches us that even in the darkest of times, we can find the strength to endure and maintain our faith.

So, my final insight is this: Embrace the unseen, understand your inner landscape, and hold onto your faith. Through these actions, you can uncover the hidden depths of life's beauty and purpose, even amidst its most challenging moments. Therefore: hold onto God's Unchanging Hand friends...Until we meet again

Supporting Sciptures for Section V

Here are a variety of resources that will guide and lead you when working with broken individuals:

The Bible offers profound wisdom and encouragement for those experiencing brokenness and seeking resilience. Here are some scriptures that provide hope and strength in times of adversity, emphasizing the unyielding spirit that emerges from trusting in God:

Psalm 34:18 (NIV) "The Lord is close to the brokenhearted and saves those who are crushed in spirit."

In moments of brokenness, this verse reminds us that God draws near to comfort and uplift those who are hurting. He is a source of solace and healing for the brokenhearted, offering hope and restoration to the weary soul.

Isaiah 41:10 (NIV) "So do not fear, for I am with you; do not be dismayed, for I am your God. I will strengthen you and help you; I will uphold you with my righteous right hand."

This powerful promise from God assures us that, in times of brokenness, we need not be afraid. His presence sustains us and empowers us to face challenges with unwavering courage.

2 Corinthians 4:8-9 (NIV) "We are hard pressed on every side, but not crushed; perplexed, but not in despair; persecuted, but not abandoned; struck down, but not destroyed."

This passage acknowledges the trials we may face in life, but it emphasizes that through God's grace, we can remain unbroken and resilient. Even in the face of adversity, our faith in Him gives us the strength to endure.

Psalm 147:3 (NIV) "He heals the brokenhearted and binds up their wounds."

God is the ultimate healer of brokenness. This verse assures us that His love and compassion are available to mend our wounds and bring restoration to our spirits.

Romans 5:3-4 (NIV) "Not only so, but we also glory in our sufferings because we know that suffering produces perseverance; perseverance, character; and character, hope.

This scripture highlights the transformative power of resilience. Through the process of enduring trials, we develop perseverance, and through perseverance, our character is strengthened, leading to a steadfast hope in God's faithfulness.

Philippians 4:13 (NIV) "I can do all this through him who gives me strength.

In times of brokenness, this verse reminds us that our strength does not come from our own abilities but from God, who empowers us to overcome challenges and embrace resilience. These scriptures affirm the unyielding spirit that emerges from trusting in God during times of brokenness. They offer hope, comfort, and encouragement, reminding us that we are never alone, and that through God's strength, we can face life's complexities with unwavering resilience.